Hawaii
The Big Island
Hiking Trails

Craig Chisholm

The Fernglen Press
473 Sixth Street
Lake Oswego, Oregon 97034

Maps: Courtesy of U.S. Geological Survey with overlays by the author.

Cover Photo: New Black Sand Beach

Design and Typesetting by L.grafix, Portland, Oregon
Printed by Lynx Communications Group, Inc., Salem, Oregon
Printed in the United States of America

Publisher's Cataloging In Publication

Chisholm, Craig.
 Hawaii, the Big Island, Hiking Trails / Craig Chisholm. —
 p. cm.
 Includes bibliographical references and index.
 ISBN 0-9612630-4-0

 1. Hiking—Hawaii—Hawaii Island—Guide-books.   2. Trails—Hawaii—
Hawaii Island—Guide-books,   3. Hawaii Island (Hawaii)—Description and
travel—1981- —Guide-books.   I. Title.

 GV199.42.H32   919.69'044
                                       QBI91-418

Trail to Thurston Lava Tube

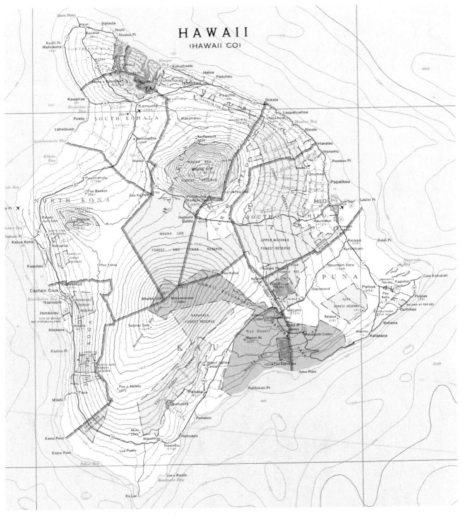

Island of Hawaii

Contents

● easiest ● easier harder ● hardest

Puu Oo Vent

Summit Caldera of Mauna Loa

Ohia Lehua Trees and Hapuu Ferns

Steam Vents — the Sulphur Banks Trail

Steam from Lava Flowing into the Ocean

The Puna Coast

Kahuna Falls — Akaka Falls State Park

Waipio Valley Viewed from the West

Petroglyphs in Hawaii Volcanoes National Park

Halape after an Earthquake

Mauna Kea Viewed from Kilauea

Dedicated to

Colin Gerald Chisholm

My Father

Acknowledgments

Through the years many people have helped with this book in many ways. I would particularly like to acknowledge the assistance of the personnel of Hawaii Volcanoes National Park, Puuhonua-o-Honaunau National Historical Park, Hawaii Natural History Association, and the Hawaii State Department of Land and Natural Resources who have been most generous and thoughtful in providing information and answering questions.

Craig Chisholm

Photography by
    Craig and Eila Chisholm
    Colin Chisholm, p. 8
    Jean Chisholm, p. 115
    J.D. Griggs (U.S.G.S.), p. 6
    Hawaii Tropical Botanical
        Garden, pp. 94 and 95
    Scott Lopez (H.V.N.P.), p. 81
    Kepa Maly (H.V.N.P.), p. 35
Edited by
    Eila Chisholm
Cover Design by
    L.grafix, Portland, Oregon

Use of the Book

The first chapter is devoted to the natural history of the Hawaiian Islands, with emphasis on the "Big Island." Information pertinent to hiking on the island is set out in the second chapter. The third chapter covers arrangements and accommodations. It includes useful addresses and information regarding permits and registrations.

The trails are grouped into four hiking areas: Hawaii Volcanoes National Park, Saddle Road, Hilo Area and Hamakua Coast, and South Kona Coast. The Hawaii Volcanoes National Park trails are further grouped into four subsections. This organization was based on either road access and proximity of the trails or on land forms and climate. Each area map shows the location of roads, trailheads, and other pertinent information.

Since the area maps show the relationship and the proximity of the trails, they are useful in planning and choosing hikes. In some cases, trails can be linked for longer hikes. Some trails are best hiked one way, if hikers can arrange a ride.

The statistical summary at the beginning of each trail description gives an estimated length of time for the round-trip hike for an average hiker. The number of calories given for each hike is what an average 150 pound hiker would burn up for the complete hike. The trails have been given the rating of easiest, easier, harder, and hardest. Though this is designed to give some notion of the relative difficulty of the trails, these ratings are, of course, quite subjective. What is hard for one hiker many be easy for another. Hikers must judge their own capabilities and not exceed them.

Total mileage for the hike, round trip, is also included in the statistical summary. The calculation of trail lengths is a matter of some debate. Where it seemed appropriate the figures generally conform to existing signs and agency literature to avoid confusion.

The highest and lowest elevations reached on the trail give some idea of the physical exertion required for the trail and the weather that may be expected. Since trails may have many ups and downs between the highest and lowest points, the topographical maps in the book should be studied to gain the best understanding of the requirements of the trails.

The statistical summary gives the names of topographical maps for the area, as well as the names of the agencies within whose jurisdiction the trail lies. The addresses for these agencies are in the Arrangements and Accommodations section.

Each trail map includes portions of the United States Geological Survey (U.S.G.S.) topographical maps. They have 20 or 40-foot-contour intervals. The maps were originally at a scale of 1:24,000. However, they may have been reduced or enlarged to fit the book. All the

Old "Pulu Factory"— the Napau Crater Trail

maps are oriented with true north at the top. On Hawaii, true north lies about 11 degrees west of magnetic north, with local variations.

Trail routes have been emphasized by overlays on the U.S.G.S. maps. Trails are marked by a single line of dashes. Dirt access roads, usually 4-wheel-drive only, are marked by a double line of dashes. Paved roads are marked by a solid line.

Complete maps may be obtained by ordering, with payment in advance, from the (U.S.G.S). They are slow in responding to orders and will not take map orders over the phone. They will, however, give out the current phone numbers of private vendors who will take phone orders and promptly send maps (for a somewhat higher price). A good selection of maps and other Hawaiiana is also available at Basically Books in Hilo. See Arrangements and Accommodations chapter for addresses.

The distances, times, routes, and other facts in this book should be considered as estimates only. Descriptions of the trails can at times be subjective and, most importantly, all conditions can change.

This book, though hopefully useful and generally accurate, must not be relied upon for complete information and accuracy. Consult those within whose jurisdiction a trail lies for current and additional information. Hikers are expected to rely on their own experience, preparation, and good on-the-spot judgment for their safety.

The Hawaiian Islands

The Hawaiian Island chain stands in the center of the North Pacific Ocean 2500 miles southwest from Los Angeles, at about the same latitude as Mexico City. The island furthest south and east is Hawaii, which is also called "the Big Island."

The Big Island is the youngest and, with 4038 square miles, by far the largest of the Hawaiian Islands. Lovely Maui, next along the chain to the northwest, is the second largest. The smaller islands of Kahoolawe, Lanai, and Molokai are near Maui and were part of it before Maui subsided far back in geologic time. Oahu follows next on the chain. The best known of the islands, it includes Honolulu, with populous Waikiki Beach, large military bases, and four-fifths of the state's population. Seventy-two miles northwest of Oahu lies green and rugged Kauai, long crafted by its large streams.

The Island Cycle

Ancient Hawaiian legend relates that Pele, the goddess of volcanoes, made her early home in Kauai. Dissatisfied, she moved southeast along the chain, eventually residing in the southeastern portion of the Island of Hawaii.

Scientific theory parallels this, saying that generally the islands are younger as one moves down the chain to the southeast, with Hawaii being the youngest and most volcanically active. The scientific explanation for this is the slow northwest progression of the Mid-Pacific oceanic plate over a stationary hot area.

In this hot area a multitude of massive volcanic domes have risen under the depths of the Pacific in succession over tens of millions of years. Such mountains are formed when magma issues out of the sea floor, piling up layer upon layer of lava. The highest of these mountains, shaped like the gently sloping backs of turtles, rise above the sea, becoming islands. Like living things, each in its time is born, grows, declines, and dies.

The Big Island is still in the building phase with two especially active shield volcanoes, Mauna Loa and Kilauea. It is, in the scale of geologic time, a mere infant compared to its older sister islands. An even younger volcano, Loihi, lies to Hawaii's southeast and under three thousand feet of ocean. It is likely to break the surface to form a new island in perhaps a hundred thousand years.

As the islands rise above the sea, algae, mosses, lichens, ferns, and magnificent forests grow on what was once sterile rock. Diverse animals make them home. The plants protect the islands from wind and rain, but cause chemical decomposition of the iron-rich, porous basalt into fertile soils.

The deep vents feeding the magma chambers underlying the islands are slowly severed as the Mid-Pacific Plate and the islands move northwest. The magma chambers change their chemistry. In their later stages

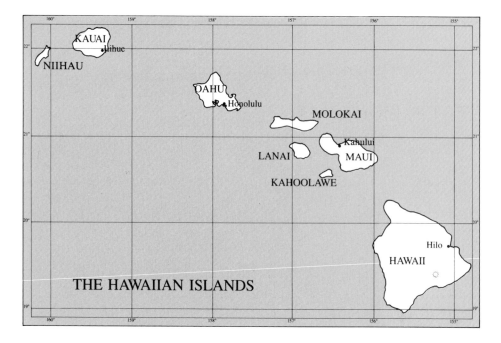

THE HAWAIIAN ISLANDS

the volcanoes add a frosting of cinder cones and volcanic ash atop their existing mass of basaltic lava flows.

Coral reefs form around the maturing islands. These living colonies of animals guard the islands against the restless ocean. However, while the coral holds the outer walls, growing up as the islands sink, erosion wears down the landward parts. The islands, no longer replenished by volcanism, lose their substance to chemical decomposition, rain, wind, and waves. Their great weight may cause them to subside and earthquakes to shear off portions. Today's high islands, now graced with abundant life, will become like the lonely, ancient, dry rocks and atolls which stretch from Kauai to Kure Atoll.

The Island of Hawaii

Pele must be happy among the Big Island's five volcanoes: Kohala, in the north, old and eroded; snow-capped Mauna Kea and Mauna Loa in the center, north and south; Hualalei on the west; and rapidly growing Kilauea against the southeast flank of also active Mauna Loa. Kilauea is so young that it has not yet built up a large,

separate cone, though it has a huge summit caldera.

Volcanic outpourings are building up the island of Hawaii faster than it is being eroded away. Thus, symmetrical volcanic domes are the most prominent landforms of the island. The Big Island shows the landscape of a volcanic island in its youth: high mountains (nearly 14,000 feet), vast fields of barren lava, active volcanic vents, lava tubes, fresh craters, and plants pioneering onto scorched, newly created land.

The deep valleys and high sea cliffs found on the other islands are absent, except along the wet windward slopes and wave-battered sea cliffs of ancient Kohala and, to a lesser degree, of somewhat younger Mauna Kea. Up along the Hamakua Coast from Hilo, on Mauna Kea's flank, are spectacular valleys and waterfalls. The Waipio-Waimanu Trail follows the rugged seacoast of Kohala, between sunken, green valleys filled with deep alluvial soils deposited by large streams cascading down high cliffs.

Since Hawaii has 63 percent of the land area of the Hawaiian Islands, its trails are often longer than those on the other islands. The scale of the mountains and the scenery

23

is far larger. However, since Hawaii has not yet experienced the full effects of erosion and much of what has taken place is covered with new layers of lava and ash, the trails are usually more gently sloping than trails on the other islands.

Large areas, especially in the west and south, are quite barren. The rain-bearing northeast trade winds are blocked from them by the high mountains. Water-holding soil has usually not yet formed on the fresh lava.

Prior to man's arrival much more of the island was forested than today. Dryland forests extended to the sea and, in wetter areas with deeper soils, great trees covered the land. In large part these have been destroyed by grazing animals and agriculture. Fields and grasslands lie in their place. Much of the ohia forest is still intact since it tends to be in regions little suited to farming and ranching.

Active examples of the geologic processes that formed all of the Hawaiian Islands are found in Hawaii Volcanoes National Park. The Kilauea Iki Trail leads into one of the most volcanically active parts of the world, over still-cooling lava, and past a volcanic vent. The Kipuka Puaulu Trail leads through another type of volcanic phenomenon, the kipuka, which is an area undamaged by surrounding flows of lava. Protected by rough surrounding lava from some of the worst depredations of livestock, kipukas provide good opportunities to observe rare native Hawaiian plants and birds.

The trails up Mauna Loa to the top of the world's largest volcano are more like mountain climbs than hikes since they lead into high, frigid regions almost devoid of life. Careful preparation is required because the cold can be extreme and there is danger of mountain sickness and serious sunburn. The high elevation to which these trails climb and the distances they cover make them exhausting. However, the grand scenes are a sufficient reward for the effort.

Ecological Change

Until man reached the Hawaiian Islands fifteen hundred years ago species new to the islands had established themselves only at long intervals. The wind bore spores of lichens and ferns. Birds flew to the islands along with whatever stuck to their feathers or was carried in their digestive systems. Floating seeds drifted to the islands' shores.

Isolated for millions of years, these species developed into diverse forms, filling the various empty ecological niches in the islands. Insects, birds, and plants multiplied and evolved until the vast majority of them became endemic. Plants such as ohia lehua established a multiplicity of forms, from tall trees to tiny bog shrubs. Snails evolved into unique sub-species on different ridges of the same island.

The terrestrial life forms that could transit the great distances from their original homes and establish themselves in the Hawaiian Islands happily left their enemies and competitors behind. They lost many of their defenses, which under their new, advantageous circumstances became unnecessary burdens. Birds became flightless. Plants lost their thorns, poisons, tough roots, and vigorous regenerative powers. This defenselessness would be their undoing.

The first wave of ecological destruction began with the pigs, dogs, rats, plants, diseases, and insects brought by the Polynesians. Species of flightless birds that once populated the islands must have fallen easy prey to dogs and hunters. Endemic plants were crowded out by introduced species. The dry-land forests that once extended to the seashores were burned off. Core samples from layers of alluvium in stream valleys tell the sad story.

The second wave of destruction began with Captain Cook's landing in 1778. From Cook's discovery followed broad and continuous commerce to all parts of the world. The gentle life forms which pre-dated man and survived the influences brought by the Polynesians now faced a host of newly imported life forms: diseases, worms, insects, voracious livestock, predators, and aggressive species of plants. Vast portions of the original habitat were destroyed by wild-fire, agriculture, and development. Whole species of endemic and indigenous plants, and the animals which depended upon them, became extinct—a complete and irretrievable evil. The cattle, goats, sheep, horses, and large European pigs introduced by early sailing ships ranged into wetter areas where they stripped the land of vegetation and laid it open to erosion.

Domestic and wild livestock were steadily destroying the forested areas on all the islands until the early 1900's. When the water supplies needed by the sugar industry became imperilled, forest areas were set aside for protection and the wild cattle were destroyed. Sugar plantation interests and government agencies began to plant previously wasted areas with introduced species of trees: Norfolk Island pine, ironwood, eucalyptus, sugi, redwood, and many others.

Some of the trails described in this book lead through such plantings, now grown into large forests. Other trails lead to wondrous places which are difficult to reach and, therefore, still have most of their original plants and animals. Unfortunately, even in such places, the agents of extinction are a threat. The conservation efforts of governmental agencies, enlightened private landowners, and organizations such as The Hawaii Nature Conservancy give a basis for hope. With proper management much can be done to preserve and even restore Hawaii's unique and rich natural legacy.

Climate and Topography

The rainfall patterns in the Hawaiian Islands vary markedly from windward to leeward. If the weather is poor for hiking, one can usually drive to a drier leeward location. Location, not season, is the prime determinant of the weather. The Pacific Ocean is cooled around Hawaii by currents originating off Alaska. Its immensity minimizes seasonal change and moderates the temperatures of the trade winds, which blow steadily from the northeast, and the Kona winds blowing from the south.

Thurston Lava Tube

Winter generally tends to be wetter. It is a few degrees cooler than summer. Summer has, at most, two and a half hours more sunlight than winter.

The trade winds, strongest in summer, passing over the rugged terrain, create distinct, almost invariable lines between microclimates. As the trade winds rise over the central mountains of the high mountainous islands, they cool to form clouds which release their moisture, most heavily on the north and northeast of each island at 2-4,000 feet. The warm, humid Kona winds from the south may occasionally vary the direction of the weather. These winds can bring extremely heavy rains, usually in winter, to all portions of the islands. Occasionally, hurricanes hit the islands.

Hiking on the Big Island

Weather

The prevailing northeast trades cause high rainfall on the windward side of the Big Island, especially near Hilo and against the Kohala Mountains. Morning and evening showers are common. The leeward, Kona, side is rainier than on other islands because the massive mountains create their own weather, drawing in rain clouds from the sea in the afternoon. On the windward side, winter and spring are wetter than summer. The Kilauea Summit area, at 4,000 feet, can be cool and wet. Snows on Mauna Loa and Mauna Kea collect in winter, but usually do not stay on the ground through summer. Temperatures drop roughly three degrees per thousand foot rise in elevation. If it is a pleasant 80 degrees at the shore, expect the top of Mauna Loa to be 38 degrees or less.

Hikers can choose weather by picking the right location at the right time. For example, windward hikes, such as the trail into the Waimanu Valley, are most prone to flooding and rain in winter and spring. During those times the coast of Hawaii Volcanoes National Park (H.V.N.P.) can be balmy and bright with fresh greenery, whereas it may be hot and parched in summer. The hikes in the Saddle Road area tend to be wet in the afternoon, as do those on the Kona side of the island. It is wisest to check the forecast, call ahead, and be flexible as to the locations of hikes.

Equipment and Clothing

Relatively little equipment is needed for most hikes in the Hawaiian Islands. The trails on the Big Island, however, are often longer than elsewhere in the islands and lead into areas with greater extremes of hot and cold. On the high mountains of the Big Island sub-freezing temperatures combine with high winds and cold rain or snow. Both cold and severe sunburn are potential dangers. Mountaineering clothing and equipment are necessary. At the other extreme, heat-stroke is a danger along the Puna Coast.

For hikes at the elevation of the Kilauea Visitor Center and on the Saddle Road a sweater may be needed. Shorts and light weight clothing are usually adequate on hikes at lower elevations. Near the sea sunglasses and a light hat with a brim are especially useful. Many visitors from less sunny regions are likely to receive painful sunburns. It is best to wear clothing that blocks the sun. Sunblock may prevent burns, but still does not stop all harmful frequencies of light.

In dry areas, especially in Hawaii Volcanoes National Park, hikers should be sure to carry extra water. Rain gear near sea level is optional; some prefer to hike in light clothing, get wet in the warm rain, and dry out later. Trails on the Big Island often cross rough aa lava. Thus, stout, broken-in boots are generally best. Sneakers may be adequate for short hikes.

Long pants guard against both brush and sunburn.

Tents are generally required for camping in campgrounds. They help to bar mosquitoes, ants, and sundry crawly pests, which are particularly troublesome at lower elevations. Insect repellent, ground pads, water bottles, first aid kit, matches for emergencies, extra food, knife, compass, maps, and the usual emergency and first aid gear should be carried. Light sleeping bags of the newer synthetic materials which hold heat even if wet are best. A flashlight (with an extra bulb) is especially important on late afternoon hikes.

Precautions

The Big Island trails usually lack water and are sometimes hot. The high climbs, above 8,000 feet, warrant precautions familiar to mountaineers. Mountain sickness is particularly common, because of the rapid rise to a high elevation. It is always unpleasant and can be serious. It does not improve with time. The only immediate cure is descent.

STAY ON THE MARKED TRAIL. Night descends rapidly because of the low latitude. This can come as a disturbing surprise to hikers from regions farther from the equator. Allow ample time in order to reach destinations before nightfall. Volcanic rock is universally rotten or weak. Therefore, cliffs in Hawaii are not suitable for rock climbing. Treacherous portable handholds abound. Vegetation may crowd in and hide drop-offs, holes, and cracks. It is a good idea to be aware of hunting in an area and to wear bright clothing. If you wander off the trail, over-optimistic hunters may mistake you for game, to their disappointment and your misfortune.

Know where you came from at all times. If a trail dwindles away you may have missed a turn. Backtrack until you are sure you are on the main trail, then look for the turnoff you missed. Likewise, if you miss an ahu (stone cairn),

Pahoehoe Lava and Fault Blocks — Puna Coast

go back to the previous one and look again.

In Hawaii Volcanoes National Park fresh lava has been little tested by time; thus, a hiker's weight may be enough to trigger a collapse into hidden cracks and caves, a misfortune greatest if one is travelling alone. Volcanic eruptions can be extremely dangerous, with a nasty fallout of fumes, cinders, and Pele's hair downwind. FOLLOW THE OFFICIAL WARNINGS and do not enter closed areas. The dangers are not always apparent. The warnings are the sum of sad experience.

Hike in company. A minor sickness or injury can become a major problem if no friend can walk out to get help. Leave your plans with a responsible person. Obtain appropriate permits and register for backcountry hiking. Carry water and treat water sources. Streams, which are found only on the slopes of the older volcanoes, may be contaminated by animals or ignorant humans upstream.

Rain, even far upstream, may make stream fords impassable or cause dangerous flash floods. Wait philosophically for waters to recede, which usually takes only a few hours of patience. Beware of falling rocks in waterfalls and alongside cliffs, especially during rainstorms.

Some plants can be poisonous if eaten, used for cooking skewers, or rubbed into the skin. Poison oak and poison ivy are not found on the Hawaiian Islands. However, the mango tree can cause a similar reaction with some people. The bark of the paper bark tree is highly irritating when wet and should not be used as toilet paper. Unless you know the fruits and berries, it is best not to eat them.

A pleasant part of hiking in Hawaii is that there are relatively few problems from animals. There are no snakes on the Big Island. Wild pigs, though shy, may attack if harmed. Mosquitoes can be a nuisance, though they are not as suicidally ferocious as some mainland varieties. They are comparative newcomers to the Hawaiian Islands. Relatively few species are present and no species has yet established itself at elevations above about 4,000 feet. All species tend to avoid strong sunlight and windy areas. Flies can be a nuisance in some areas. Crawly creatures such as centipedes, scorpions, black widow spiders and a few other unpleasant invertebrates may be found, but not often and usually only at lower elevations. Mongooses, mice, rats, and feral cats often help themselves to unsecured food. Tents with mosquito netting neutralize most problems.

Hikers following the sea coast should not be lulled into thinking that all waves are the same size. Combinations of the amplitudes of two or more waves may create "rogue" waves. These are much larger than the usual waves and occasionally sweep the unwary into the sea.

Earthquakes on the Pacific Rim cause multiple tsunami waves many hours later, far away in Hawaii. Warnings of these may be given by the authorities. At rare intervals strong or long local earthquakes on Kilauea cause sudden tsunami. The only hope of avoiding these is to run uphill immediately at the shock of the earthquake. Sharks in the waters off the beaches are not noted for being man-eaters; however, some may be unaware of this general rule. Various smaller sea creatures, waves, and currents are a far greater danger. Tube worm cases, urchins, and other creatures may injure the feet of waders.

Emergency services can be reached by telephoning 911. Crime and violence exist in Hawaii as elsewhere, though statistics indicate that the crime rate is lower than the United States average. Nonetheless, the same precautions should be followed as on the mainland. Just because Hawaii is a paradise, hikers and especially campers, particularly adjacent to roads and populous areas, should not think themselves immune from theft and other crimes. Just as on the mainland, women should not camp and travel alone. Violent crime is unusual. Thefts are more common, especially in areas frequented by tourists. Valuables should not be left unattended in tents or locked in cars.

Marijuana patches, though now less common, must be strictly avoided since they may be jealously and dangerously guarded. They are usually carefully hidden from the authorities and anyone else and are not likely to be found along well-travelled trails. This is yet another reason to stay on the known trails. As a practical matter, the hazards of driving and sunburn, though prosaic, are far more likely to cause problems than the hazards of crime.

Fires

Open fires are not permitted in the back country. Even at campsites next to paved roads open fires are prohibited, except at a few designated fireplaces.

In Hawaii Volcanoes National Park,

Nene Geese at Kipuka Nene

fires are prohibited other than in the pavilion fireplaces at Namakani Paio and Kipuka Nene camping area and Kipuka Puaulu. This is for good reason: the fire danger is simply too great. Introduced grasses provide fuel for fires that threaten native species not well adapted to fire. In any case, campfires in the warm lowland climate add little comfort and at higher, cooler elevations firewood is scarce or damp. Smoking while hiking is strictly prohibited. Hilina Pali Road is sometimes closed because of fire danger.

Use camp stoves or, better yet, do not bother to cook. Fuel must be purchased locally, since airlines sensibly forbid it on planes. The most practical course in the back country is to travel light and dispense with the nuisance of fire making and cooking altogether.

Conservation Issues

The usual admonitions regarding minimal-impact camping and hiking apply in Hawaii: pack out what you bring in, damage nothing, and do not contaminate water with soap and suntan oils. In short, leave nature as you found it. Clean your shoes and equipment before you leave one area for another, especially when travelling to another island. Unless you do so, you may become the unwitting carrier of noxious weed seeds into areas formerly unspoiled. Do not trench around tents.

The National Park Service, the Division of Forestry and Wildlife, and the Division of State Parks take care of the trails, shelters, plants, and animals of the back country. The brushing, marking, fire fighting, cleaning, and repairing seen along the trails is their work. The personnel of these departments are keenly aware of all that needs to be protected and are remarkably dedicated to the task. It is an unfortunate fact that a major part of their efforts must be diverted to cleaning up litter and repairing damage by vandals. Whatever hikers can do to assist in eliminating litter, fire, and vandalism is of considerable benefit to the environment since it will free up resources for the critical tasks of protecting nature in Hawaii.

Arrangements and Accommodations

All the trails described in this book are accessible to the public. The trails are all on lands administered by Hawaii Volcanoes National Park (H.V.N.P.), Hawaii Division of Forestry and Wildlife, or Hawaii Division of State Parks, except for the trail in Hawaii Botanical Garden, which is managed by a non-profit foundation.

Day hiking permits are not ordinarily required on these trails. Hawaii Volcanoes National Park charges a modest admission fee, used for park administration. The hike to the Napau Crater in H.V.N.P. requires a permit because of current volcanic activity. Kilauea Visitor Center (park headquarters) is open daily from 7:45 a.m. to 4:45 p.m. for registration and permits. Hawaii Botanical Garden has an admission charge.

Camping and use of cabins require reservations or permits from the governmental agency in charge. These are either free or inexpensive.

For permits, reservations, materials, and current information concerning hiking, camping, cabin use, and related subjects consult the entities listed below for their current requirements. Speak to them well in advance to be sure of reservations. These governmental agencies also provide free, useful literature on the lands under their jurisdiction. Allow time for mailing.

Addresses for Information

National Parks

National Park Service
300 Ala Moana Blvd., Suite 6305
P.O. Box 50165
Honolulu, HI 96850
(808) 546-7584

Kilauea Visitor Center
Hawaii Volcanoes National Park
P.O. Box 52
Hawaii National Park, HI 96718-0052
(808) 967-7311
(808) 967-7977 (eruption info.)

Puuhonua-o-Honaunau National Historical Park
Honaunau, Kona, HI 96726
(808) 328-2288

Volcano House
P.O. Box 53
Hawaii National Park, HI 96718-0053
(808) 967-7321

Forest and Natural Area Reserves

Division of Forestry and Wildlife
Department of Land and Natural Resources
P.O. Box 4849, 1643 Kilauea Avenue
Hilo, HI 96720-0849
(808) 933-4221

State Parks
Division of State Parks
Department of Land and Natural
Resources
P.O. Box 936, 75 Aupuni Street
Hilo, HI 96721-0936
(808) 933-4200

County Beach Parks
Department of Parks and Recreation
County of Hawaii
25 Aupuni Street
Hilo, HI 96720
(808) 961-8311

Topographic Maps and Nature Books
U.S. Geological Survey
Branch of Distribution
Box 25286, Denver Federal Center
Denver, CO 80225
(303) 236-7477

Basically Books
46 Waianuenue Avenue
Hilo, HI 96720
(808) 961-0144

Kilauea Visitor Center
Hawaii Volcanoes National Park
P.O. Box 52
Hawaii National Park, HI 96718-0052
(808) 967-7311

Hawaii Tropical Botanical Garden
RR 143-A
Papaikou, HI 96781
(808) 964-5233

Bus Schedules
Mass Transportation Agency
Hele-On Bus
25 Aupuni Street
Hilo, HI 96720
(808) 935-8241

Volunteering on Trails
Na Ala Hele Trails and Access System
Kawaiahao Plaza, Suite 132
567 South King Street
Honolulu, HI 96813
(808) 587-0058

Bed and Breakfasts
Bed and Breakfast Hawaii
P.O. Box 449
Kaapa, Kauai, HI 96746
(808) 742-6995

Cabins, Shelters, and Campsites

Cabins, shelters, and campsites are available through the Division of State Parks, the Division of Forestry and Wildlife, Hawaii Volcanoes National Park, or the County of Hawaii.

Campgrounds near roads can almost always be reached by two-wheel-drive cars, even in wet weather, since there is little mud in most parts of the Big Island. Water must be packed in to the back country and to many roadside campsites. Treat catchment system water and ground water. No open fires, only backpacking stoves, are allowed in the backcountry.

Hawaii Volcanoes National Park (H.V.N.P.) has A-frame cabins for those Sybarites who insist on warm water and beds. With linens from Volcano House and communal showers they offer reasonable comfort for a relatively modest price. The cabins are at Namakani Paio Campground on Highway 11, three miles west of Kilauea Visitor Center. Reservations are required and can be obtained from Volcano House. Historic Volcano House on the rim of Kilauea Caldera has the customary hotel facilities. Information regarding lodgings in the nearby village of Volcano is also available from the park. For military personnel, Kilauea Military Camp, a mile west on the rim from the visitor center, has comfortable cabins and eating facilities.

The only drive-in campgrounds in the park are Namakani Paio on Highway 11 and Kipuka Nene on Hilina Pali Road.

Namakani Paio has piped water, fireplaces, and toilet facilities. Its communal showers are for cabin occupants only. Kipuka Nene has catchment water, a pavilion, and a pit toilet. Stays are limited to 7 days per campground, per year, on a first-come basis. The campground may be closed during Nene nesting season (November through March).

Backcountry camping requires permits. They are issued free at Kilauea Visitor Center no earlier than noon of the day before the hike, on a first-come basis. Groups are limited to 8 persons in some sites and 12 in others and stays to 3 nights per site. When registering check on catchment water level at the cabins and shelters.

The East and Southwest Rift Zones have limited camping. Napau Crater campsite, at the end of the Napau Crater Trail, has only pit toilets and neither water nor shelter. Kipuka Pepeiao Cabin borders the Kau Desert, near the top of the pali above the coast, 4.8 miles beyond the end of the Hilina Pali Road. It has three bunks, catchment water, and pit toilets. Groups are limited to 12 persons and stays to 3 nights per site.

The Coastal Region has three seaside campsites and primitive three-walled shelters: Keauhou on the Puna Coast Trail, Halape at the end of the Puna Coast and Halape Trails, and Kaaha on the Kaaha Trail. A total of 16 persons are allowed at each coastal site. There are water catchment tanks and pit toilets at these campsites. Generally tent camping near the shelters makes the most sense.

Mauna Loa has two cabins. Puu Ulaula, also called Red Hill Cabin, is at 10,035 feet, 7.5 miles up the Mauna Loa Trail. It has 8 bunks with mattresses. Mauna Loa Cabin, at 13,250 feet on the east rim of Mokuaweoweo Caldera, is the terminus of both routes described in this book. It has 12 bunks with mattresses.

Division of Forestry and Wildlife maintains a shelter about two-thirds of the way along the Waipio-Waimanu Valleys (Muliwai) Trail. Camping is also allowed near the black sand beach in Waimanu.

State Parks require permits and modest fees for all camping and cabin use. Cabins at Mauna Kea State Recreation Area (Pohakuloa) along the Saddle Road on Mauna Kea are at a usually dry and cool 6,500-foot elevation. Cabins and a campground at Kalopa State Park in the rainy Hamakua region are at about 2,000 feet. Both parks are quite conveniently near trails described in this book. Kilauea State Recreation Area near H.V.N.P. has one cabin. There are 4-person A-frame shelters at Hapuna Beach State Recreation Area.

County Beach Parks, under the jurisdiction of the Department of Parks and Recreation of the County of Hawaii, are at frequent intervals adjacent to the highways which follow the coast. They require permits and modest fees for camping. Thirteen of the parks have campsites, of varying quality. These are usually far removed from the better hiking areas, can be somewhat crowded, and have a less favorable reputation for public order than national park camping areas.

Conventional Lodgings

It is easy to find handsome lodgings on the island of Hawaii, but at handsome prices. Simple economy motels can be found away from the main tourist haunts. Remember that even "the Big Island" is small enough that it is feasible to stay in one area and drive to hike in another. Thus, hiking can be combined with other interests, such as, sightseeing, shopping, and enjoying beach activities, an important consideration when travelling with companions with varied interests.

The Manago Hotel in Captain Cook is quite reasonable and has an exceptionally good dining room. There are a number of bed and breakfast organizations, the largest being Bed and Breakfast Hawaii.

A good general guide book to the Hawaiian Islands is well worth obtaining to complement this book. Check out publica-

A-frame Cabins — Namakani Paio Campground

tions, such as, *Paradise Family Guides, Fodor's Hawaii, Hidden Hawaii,* and *Birnbaum's Hawaii.* They contain current phone numbers, prices, and other details concerning lodging, restaurants, and many other matters.

Transportation

Reduced fares may be available on inter-island jet flights for military, stand-by, youth, or off-hour fliers, holders of commuter tickets, and passengers with tickets purchased in connection with flights from outside the state. Check with your travel agent. Military flights are occasionally made from Oahu.

Daily bus transportation is available on the main highways. Car rental clerks, observing camping gear, occasionally refuse to rent to campers without proof of reservations at a hotel. Car rental contracts for passenger cars may contain clauses prohibiting the use of cars on unpaved roads or on the Saddle Road and, thus, voiding insurance if so used. Do not leave valuables in cars.

Bicycles are permitted on highways, even when there are no bikeways, and they are subject to laws governing other vehicles. Biking on the Big Island is difficult because of the long distances, narrow shoulders, and considerable changes in elevation. If you plan to bike, write to Hawaii Police Department, 349 Kapiolani Street, Hilo, HI 96720 for information on licensing, insurance, and other requirements. Mountain bikes are not permitted on the trails in Hawaii Volcanoes National Park. Generally the trails in Hawaii are too rough for mountain bikes. Hitchhiking can be dangerous because of the narrow shoulders on roads.

Hawaii Volcanoes National Park (H.V.N.P.)

Hawaii Volcanoes National Park (H.V.N.P.), on the southeast side of the island, has within its boundaries remarkable variety. In elevation it extends from the cold, thin air atop 13,677-foot-high Mauna Loa down to Kilauea, the other active volcano in the park, at 4,000 feet, and to the hot seacoast of Puna and Kau. Vegetation also varies greatly.

The park entrance is 30 miles southwest of Hilo on Highway 11, and 95 miles from Kailua-Kona on Highway 11 going around the south of the island. There is a modest admission fee to enter the park. Park headquarters is in the same building as Kilauea Visitor Center near the park entrance. They are open daily from 7:45 a.m. to 4:45 p.m., telephone (808) 967-7311 or, for eruption information, (808) 967-7977. Kilauea Visitor Center has interpretive displays, a theater showing films about the park, and a bookstore run by the Hawaii Natural History Association. Rangers issue permits, lead hikes, and provide information about the park.

The H.V.N.P. trails described in this book are grouped into four sections: Kilauea Summit, Southwest and East Rift Zones, Coastal Region, and Mauna Loa Climbs.

The trails in the Kilauea Summit section are in the center of the park around Kilauea Caldera (also referred to as Kilauea Crater on U.S.G.S. maps). Close to roads, this is the most frequently visited area. At 4,000 feet above sea level the weather around Kilauea Caldera is generally mild but can be chilly and damp any time of year. Kilauea Visitor Center and Volcano House are on the northeast rim of the caldera.

The Southwest and East Rift Zones extend out from Kilauea Caldera and are geologically similar. However, while the East Rift Zone is forest-covered, the Southwest Rift Zone is a desert. Not only is the Southwest Rift Zone drier, but the rain it does receive mixes with fumes from the volcanic vents to windward and becomes acid rain.

The Coastal Region, below the rift zones, is hot and dry much of the year. Kilauea's slope steepens here because of the massive faults formed as the mountain side slips down to a flat coastal plain. In the scale of geologic time, this region is often flooded by lava coming down from the rift zones.

The Mauna Loa Climbs section includes two trails which lead to the great summit caldera, Mokuaweoweo. The weather high on Mauna Loa can be cold, with high winds and snow, quite unlike what is expected in Hawaii.

Be sure to read the earlier section on Precautions, page 27.

East Rift Spatter Cone — Kilauea

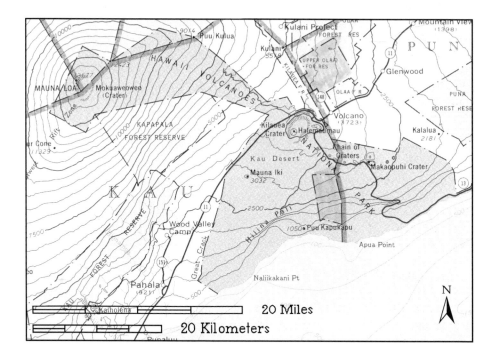

Kilauea Summit

Kilauea Volcano lies in low profile against the southeast flank of huge Mauna Loa. Both shield volcanoes have distinct roots, as evidenced by their independent eruptions. They are among the most active, but least explosive, volcanoes in the world, to the great interest of volcanologists, the delight of tourists and hikers, and the frustration of road builders.

The relatively fluid lava which builds Hawaiian volcanoes comes from deep in the earth's crust and contains a high percentage of metals and relatively little gas. Lava floods out in rivers from Hawaiian volcanoes to form lava shields with only about six degree slopes. The spectacular cliffs found further up the chain are the products of later erosion or faulting.

"Kilauea Summit" is not a traditional steep mountain top. It is simply the highest place on the gentle slopes of young, little-eroded Kilauea shield volcano, scarcely noticeable when approached from a distance. The summit's central feature is awesome Kilauea Caldera, a two-mile wide lake-like expanse of black, hardened lava, ringed by high cliffs, and containing within it the fuming crater, Halemaumau. Such formations result from the collapse of the mountain as underlying magma flows out from rifts further down the slopes.

Trails described in this section circle the caldera, descend into it, or visit nearby points of interest. Along these trails hikers are treated to sights of tree molds, cracks, craters, steam vents, and lava flows. Some of the trails pass through lovely ohia and fern forests, which ebb and flow over time as they are destroyed by the volcano and then again spread over devastated lands.

The Sulphur Banks Loop, Iliahi Loop, and Earthquake-Caldera Floor Loop near Kilauea Visitor Center are short, forested trails offering much of interest. The Halemaumau-Byron Ledge Loop crosses the flat, barren floor of Kilauea Caldera to a view of smoldering Halemaumau, the sulfurous heart of the volcano. The Kilauea Iki Loop leads by the mouth of a still-cooling volcanic vent, which created Puu Puai Cinder Cone during the spectacular 1959 eruption. The nearby Devastation Trail is an easy walk along the ash-covered side of Puu Puai. The Crater Rim Trail makes a long circuit of the caldera, a sort of grand tour of volcanism. Kipuka Puaulu (Bird Park) Trail offers sights of animal life and native Hawaiian forest in a kipuka, an area spared from surrounding lava flows.

Camping is available at Namakani Paio (3,900 feet, water tank, toilets, fireplaces, and hard ground), a somewhat cool and wet forested grove 3 miles west on Highway 11 from Kilauea Visitor Center. In addition to hotel accommodations, Volcano House provides cabins at Namakani Paio Campground.

Halemaumau Crater

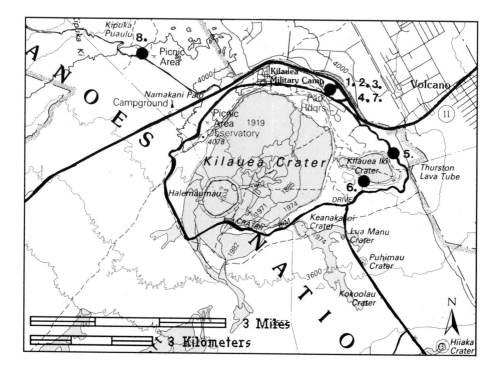

1. Sulphur Banks Loop

Kilauea Summit
1 hour, loop trip
140 calories; easiest
1.6 miles, loop trip
Highest point: 3980 feet
Lowest point: 3925 feet
Map: Kilauea Crater 1:24,000,
Hawaii Volcanoes National Park

This easy loop is made up of the Sulphur Banks Trail on the outward leg and a segment of the Crater Rim Trail on the return portion. Steam vents surrounded by light yellow deposits of sulfur, open fields underlain by hot rock, and a walk through ohia forest atop Kilauea Caldera's rim are features of this route. The steam vents are most impressive during the cooler parts of humid days and when the sun is low, making this a fine hike for a cool, rainy day.

Most steam vents around Kilauea Caldera are caused by rain water touching hot rocks. This produces almost pure steam or water vapor. Such steam vents smell little of sulfur. Ferns and mosses grow in luxury close to them, enjoying perpetual warmth and humidity.

The vents at Sulphur Banks, however, are bare of vegetation. The topography of the area indicates that these vents follow the edge of a much older Kilauea Caldera. The faults beneath the vents must reach far down toward the underlying magma. From the magma comes substantial quantities of sulfur dioxide (SO2), sulfur vapor and, in small quantities, poisonous hydrogen sulphide (H2S) with its smell of rotten eggs. Bright yellow, elemental sulfur is deposited at the cool surface.

Route: The trailhead is near the west side of Kilauea Visitor Center's parking lot. The trail leads west, paralleling the right hand (north) side of Crater Rim Drive along a grassy route by hapuu (tree

Steam Vents

ferns) and koa trees. At 0.1 miles the trail forks. The left, asphalted fork, turns down to the highway, while the Sulphur Banks Trail goes right. The trail descends gently, becoming a wide, smooth path through ohia and fern forest. At 0.3 miles it comes to the Sulphur Banks viewpoint, where the odor of sulfur is noticeable. The trail continues west across an area covered by grass. It passes numerous steam vents and then goes through uluhe (staghorn fern), bamboo orchids, and a generous growth

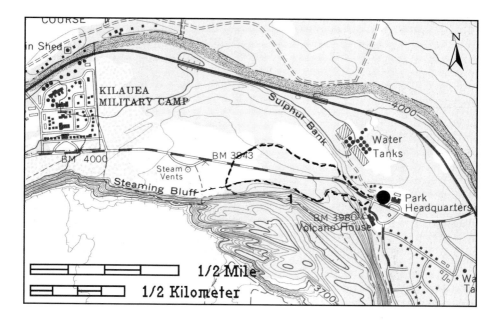

of ohelo berries. The underlying ground is too warm for trees to grow.

At 0.7 miles the trail crosses Crater Rim Drive. It soon comes to a junction with the Crater Rim Trail going left and right, and the Sandalwood Trail leading ahead to a good viewpoint of Kilauea Caldera. To continue on the Sulphur Banks Loop, go left onto the Crater Rim Trail, which parallels the caldera's rim and a long crack with steam vents. At 0.5 miles beyond this, the Crater Rim Trail reaches a junction with the Halemaumau Trail coming up from the caldera. At this junction, continue left on the Crater Rim Trail, climbing steps to return to Kilauea Visitor Center.

2. Iliahi Loop

Kilauea Summit
1 1/2 hours, loop trip
175 calories; easiest
1.5 miles, loop trip
Highest point: 3980 feet
Lowest point: 3790 feet
Map: Kilauea Crater 1:24,000
Hawaii Volcanoes National Park

The Iliahi Loop trail is made up of the Sandalwood Trail and portions of the Crater Rim and Halemaumau Trails. This popular, short hike starts from Kilauea Visitor Center, descends through a fern forest, then climbs along a cliff edge overlooking Kilauea Caldera.

The cliff edge portion of the trail, which also overlooks the canopy of an ohia forest, is particularly good for watching the small native birds in the treetops. The most common is the apapane, a five-inch-long, bright-red bird with black wings and tail. Also seen is the amakihi, a small green bird with a black eye mask. They are most active in early morning or evening.

Route: From Kilauea Visitor Center circle around the edge of the parking lot counterclockwise and cross Crater Rim Drive to a logo of a hiker, which marks a short connector trail to the Crater Rim Trail. Follow this trail, for 75 yards, paralleling Crater Rim Drive. The trail comes to an intersection with a sign showing trail mileage and directions. Follow the trail to the right, with a sign reading "Sandalwood Trail 0.3 miles." The trail soon descends steps and comes to another intersection, which is the start of the loop. Go left here on the Halemaumau Trail.

The loop first descends through a deep native forest of ohia trees, hapuu (tree ferns), and amaumau ferns. Markers along the way identify native plants. Native

Fern and Ohia Forest

birds call and cheery crickets chirp as they rub their wings to attract mates. These crickets evolved here over millions of years into a unique species with unique songs. Commit their songs to your memory while you may, for the endemic invertebrates in Hawaii also face the dangers of extinction.

After 0.2 miles take a turnoff to the right, onto the Sandalwood Trail. The trail threads its way along a cliff edge and

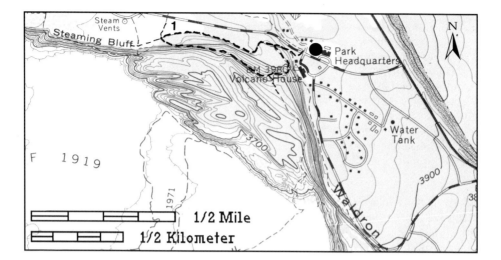

gradually climbs up to the caldera rim.
There are fine views of Puu Puai Cinder
Cone, Kilauea Caldera, and Halemaumau
Crater. The trail passes by steaming vents,
surrounded by luxuriant growths of little
ferns and mosses enjoying perpetual summer. Shortly after reaching the caldera
rim, the trail comes to an intersection of
trails, with the Crater Rim Trail running
left and right, and the Sulphur Banks Trail
straight ahead. To complete the loop, continue to the right onto the Crater Rim Trail
and follow it for 0.5 miles to the junction
you left at the bottom of the steps leading
back to Kilauea Visitor Center.

3. Earthquake—Caldera Floor Loop

Kilauea Summit
1 3/4 hours, loop trip
450 calories; easier
2.7 miles, loop trip
Highest point: 3980 feet
Lowest point: 3550 feet
Map: Kilauea Crater 1:24,000
Hawaii Volcanoes National Park

In 1975, the southeast side of Kilauea slipped toward the coast of Puna and Kau in a great earthquake. Tsunami waves swept the shore, cracks appeared inland, and rocks were shaken loose from cliffs. At that time Crater Rim Drive ran atop Waldron Ledge, close to Kilauea Caldera's rim. The earthquake opened large cracks in the road and caused portions of the rim to fall into the caldera. A subsequent local earthquake in 1983 finished the job. The park service prudently closed this section of the road to vehicles. It relocated the Crater Rim Trail away from the rim to follow the course of the closed and cracked road, leaving intact the evidence of the natural forces at work in the area.

This loop trail includes the closed portion of Crater Rim Drive along Waldron Ledge (Kaauea), and parts of the Crater Rim, Kilauea Iki, Byron Ledge, and Halemaumau Trails.

Route: From Kilauea Visitor Center walk across Crater Rim Drive to go around Volcano House on the right. Join the Crater Rim Trail behind Volcano House and continue, left, between Volcano House and the caldera rim. Pass a viewpoint shelter and reach the old course of Crater Rim Drive. Go right on the old road. The trail follows the road but skirts sections which have fallen into Kilauea Caldera. Eventually the road swings left away from the caldera while the Crater

Earthquake Crack

Rim Trail, the route to follow, goes into the forest along Waldron Ledge.

At 1.0 miles the trail comes to a junction with the Kilauea Iki Trail where there are good views of Kilauea Iki Crater and its vent, Puu Puai. Descend, right, on the Kilauea Iki Trail toward the tree fern and ohia forest on Byron Ledge. After this descent, the Kilauea Iki Trail leads left. Go straight to join the Byron Ledge Trail after a level 0.3-mile stroll through ohia forest. Turn right to switchback down 400

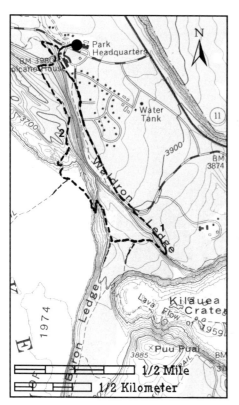

Returning Life

feet to the floor of Kilauea Caldera, which is littered with boulders shaken from the rim.

Follow the ahu (rock piles) 0.2 miles directly across the floor to join the Halemaumau Trail. Take this trail back up to the caldera rim, passing by the start of the Sandalwood Trail along the way. When the Halemaumau Trail reaches the Crater Rim Trail, turn right, up steps leading back to Kilauea Visitor Center.

For an easier variation take only the level portion of the loop, along Waldron Ledge to the junction with the Kilauea Iki Trail, and return before going down into the caldera. This portion is wheelchair accessible.

4. Halemaumau—Byron Ledge Loop
Kilauea Summit
4 hours, loop trip
1000 calories; harder
6.5 miles, loop trip
Highest point: 3980 feet
Lowest point: 3524 feet
Map: Kilauea Crater 1:24,000
Hawaii Volcanoes National Park

The Halemaumau—Byron Ledge Loop trail descends to Kilauea Caldera's lake-like floor and crosses flows of pahoehoe lava, congealed into innumerable ropey rolls and billows, to the east rim of Halemaumau Crater. Until 1924 Halemaumau contained a lake of molten lava. In that year the lake disappeared after violent steam eruptions apparently altered the vents supplying magma. Halemaumau Crater remains a sulfurous, steaming pit, providing a sobering glimpse of the hellish interior of our planet.

Early writers, such as the intrepid Scottish botanist, James Macrae, who descended from Byron Ledge in 1825 into the caldera, described a deeper caldera and scenes quite different from those seen today. The floor levels of both Kilauea and Halemaumau change greatly with the ebb and flow of underlying magma.

Route: From Kilauea Visitor Center go counterclockwise around the parking lot and cross Crater Rim Drive to a logo of a hiker, which marks a short connector trail to the Crater Rim Trail. Follow this trail, paralleling Crater Rim Drive, to an intersection where a sign shows trail mileage and directions. Take the trail to the right and immediately descend steps to another intersection, where the loop starts. Take the Halemaumau Trail, down, left, through a hapuu fern and ohia forest. Pass by a turnoff to the Sandalwood Trail on the way down and one end of the Byron Ledge Trail upon reaching the caldera floor.

Ahu (stone piles) mark the course of the Halemaumau Trail, southwest, across the level caldera floor. The route crosses pahoehoe lava flows from 1974, 1885, 1954, 1982, and, finally, 1894. Note the return of pioneering ferns, grasses, puki-awe, and ohelo bushes, which vary in thickness with the age of the flow. Keep to the trail—the pahoehoe lava has weak spots which may collapse underfoot.

At about 2.5 miles the Byron Ledge Trail comes in from the left. Continue straight ahead on the Halemaumau Trail, which climbs slightly as it nears the Halemaumau Overlook on the dangerously unstable crater rim. Steam rises from cracks all around. The air has the burning stench of sulfur.

If you have not arranged a pickup from the parking area near the overlook, return to the junction with the Byron Ledge Trail. There you may return as you came or make a loop by following the Byron Ledge Trail east to climb Byron Ledge and traverse its length. The Byron Ledge Trail goes through a pleasant ohia forest atop the ledge and passes two short side trails to Kilauea Iki Crater before it descends back onto the caldera floor. It crosses the boulder-strewn floor below Waldron Ledge and rejoins the Halemaumau Trail just as it starts the climb back up the caldera rim to Kilauea Visitor Center.

Onto Kilauea Caldera's Floor

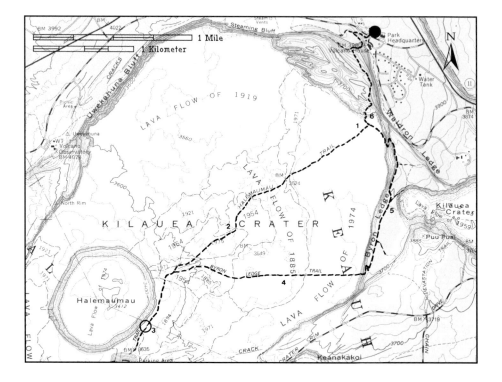

5. Kilauea Iki Loop
Kilauea Summit
2 1/2 hours, loop trip
500 calories; harder
4 miles, loop trip
Highest point: 3940 feet
Lowest point: 3500 feet
Maps: Kilauea Crater, Volcano 1:24,000
Hawaii Volcanoes National Park

Kilauea Iki, "Little Kilauea," is almost a scale model of the huge, nearby Kilauea Caldera. Both were formed when the ground collapsed as underlying magma flowed out from rifts further down the mountain. Kilauea Iki is famous for the great eruption of 1959 in which a lava fountain at one point reached 1900 feet high. Spewing from the southwest side of Kilauea Iki, it half filled the crater and put on a spectacular display for 36 days. Films of volcanic eruptions are shown at Kilauea Visitor Center. The trail crosses these scenes of volcanism, which, for the moment, are quietly cooling.

Route: Drive from Kilauea Visitor Center south, left, on Crater Rim Road for approximately 1.5 miles to the Kilauea Iki Overlook parking area. The trailhead is clearly marked at the north end of the parking lot. Walk counterclockwise along the north rim of Kilauea Iki Crater, at first following a segment of the Crater Rim Trail. About 0.7 miles from the trailhead, the Kilauea Iki Trail branches, left, off the Crater Rim Trail and descends through a handsome forest of ohia trees and hapuu tree ferns.

At the bottom of the descent it passes by one, then another connector to the Byron Ledge Trail. These connectors lead to the right to impressive views of Kilauea Caldera. From the junction with the second connector, the Kilauea Iki Trail goes down the jumbled lava on the side of Kilauea Iki

Crater to its floor and past the vent of the 1959 Puu Puai lava fountain.

Many ohelo bushes, loaded with succulent, red berries, may be found along the way. These berries are one of the earliest plants to appear after volcanic activity has scorched the ground. Tradition has it that to eat any without first paying due respect to Pele, the spirit of volcanism, may kindle her extreme displeasure. Since at this point you are about to walk across almost a mile of still-cooling lava, past a dormant volcanic vent, you might weigh this tradition carefully against your own convictions.

Beyond the vent, the trail leads across the crater's floor on flat, hardened lava, which sends up clouds of water vapor where water reaches the still hot rocks beneath the surface. Note how ferns and small mosses are slowly pioneering into this area. Proceed directly across the crater to its east side where a stone cairn marks the trail up the east wall. The trail switchbacks through a forest of giant hapuu tree ferns and ends at Crater Rim Road and a junction with the Crater Rim Trail.

Immediately across the road a short loop trail, 0.3 miles, leads to and through Thurston Lava Tube (Nahuku), a worthwhile side trip. Return to your starting point by following the Crater Rim Trail counterclockwise along the rim of Kilauea Iki for 0.5 miles.

Kilauea Iki Crater

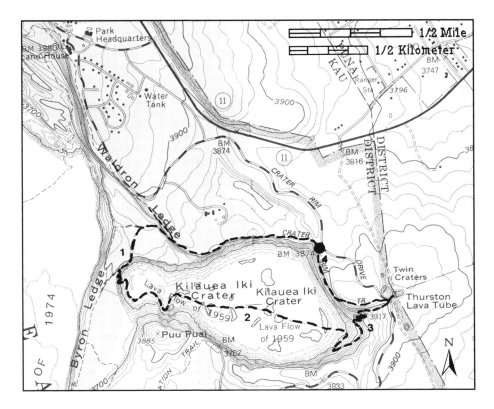

6. Devastation Trail

Kilauea Summit
3/4 hours, round trip
140 calories; easiest
1.0 miles, round trip
Highest point: 3760 feet
Lowest point: 3700 feet
Map: Kilauea Crater 1:24,000
Hawaii Volcanoes National Park

The Devastation Trail follows a paved path built on an area covered with volcanic spatter and cinders by the 1959 eruption of Kilauea Iki. The gradual return of vegetation since then demonstrates that devastation is only a part of the cycle of volcanism and regrowth. Pele, the goddess of volcanism, is associated with ohelo berries and ohia trees, allegorically connecting the processes of volcanic destruction with those of regeneration. These native plants, having adapted well to this environment, return quickly to areas covered by ash and lava.

Even on land recently devastated by volcanic activity, which is an unusual ecological niche, one can see the influences of introduced species. Newcomers, like faya tree or firetree (Myrica faya) may, in subtle ways, be changing the ancient web of life in Hawaii. Some of these weedy species have the ability to fix nitrogen. This makes the nitrogen-poor volcanic soils more suitable for them. It enables these and other newcomers to outgrow species such as ohia which formerly had an unchallenged advantage on newly created ground.

Route: From Kilauea Visitor Center drive clockwise on Crater Rim Drive for 2.9 miles to the turnoff to the Puu Puai Overlook, 1.2 miles past Thurston Lava Tube (Nahuku). Go to the overlook, where the trail begins. The trail climbs slightly, then makes a gradual descent for 15 min-

Puu Puai Cinder Cone — Buried Ohia Forest

utes along the path to the Devastation Parking Area 0.5 miles away, which can serve as a pick-up point for those wishing to shorten the hike. Along the way are interpretive signs telling the story of the destruction and regeneration apparent along the trail.

For those wanting more exercise, a half-mile-long, cinder side trail leads northwest from the south end of the Devastation Trail down to Byron Ledge and a

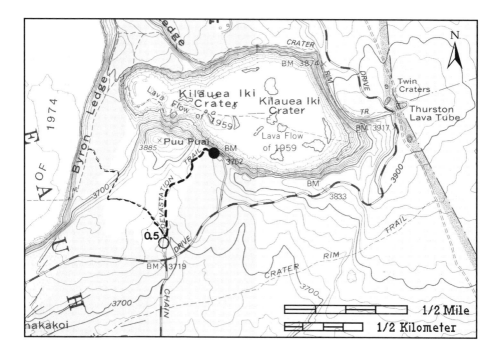

view of Kilauea Caldera. Two hundred yards down this trail are the solemn, whitened trunks of a dead ohia forest partially buried by cinders from Puu Puai.

Byron Ledge is named after Lord Byron, captain of the Blonde, which visited Hawaii in 1825. The diary of James Macrae, the ship's botanist, describes a descent into Kilauea Caldera, probably via Byron Ledge. The vegetation, topography, and volcanism described in the diary differ markedly from what is seen today. The return from Byron Ledge to the Devastation Trail requires a climb of 150 feet in elevation.

Devastation Trail in the Early Years

7. Crater Rim Trail
Kilauea Summit
8 hours, loop trip
1800 calories; harder
11.6 miles, loop trip
Highest point: 4080 feet
Lowest point: 3600 feet
Map: Kilauea Crater 1:24,000
Hawaii Volcanoes National Park

This long trail is the grand tour of Hawaiian volcanism. Its nearly level route skirts around the huge caldera of Kilauea, one of the world's most active, but least explosive, volcanoes. Lava and cinders, steam vents, rifts, craters, tree molds, a lava tube, and views of the devastation and return of life are found along the trail.

The weather varies from cool showers in the lush fern forests in the east and north to hot, dry conditions in the barren Kau Desert in the south. Carry water, since none is available along the trail, except at Thurston Lava Tube (Nahuku) and the Jaggar Museum. The trail parallels Chain of Craters Road for most of its length. Do not hike the trail at night, as it often skirts deadly, unmarked drop-offs.

Route: Walk to the west end of Kilauea Visitor Center's parking lot and across Crater Rim Drive. A short connector trail, marked by a logo of a hiker, leads through uluhe fern to the Crater Rim Trail. Turn left and walk between the caldera rim and Volcano House. The trail soon joins the abandoned course of Crater Rim Drive, which was severely cracked by earthquakes in 1975 and 1983.

After paralleling the rim of Kilauea Caldera for about a mile and leaving the old road, the trail passes by the Kilauea Iki Trail, which descends off into Kilauea Iki Crater. Follow the Crater Rim Trail along the north edge of Kilauea Iki Crater. Cross Crater Rim Drive to Thurston Lava Tube (Nahuku), a worthwhile side trip.

From Thurston Lava Tube continue the course of an old dirt road through ohia and fern forest. The trail leaves the dirt road and heads westerly to cross Chain of Craters Road. The forest becomes sparser and the trail soon reaches pahoehoe flows from the 1974 eruption near Lua Manu Crater. These thin flows of lava overran an ohia forest, reaching high up the trunks of the trees. The level of the molten lava dropped, leaving solidified lava in molds around the charred tree trunks.

As the trail enters open country, it passes just south of Keanakakoi Crater. For the next three miles it traverses the northern reaches of the Kau Desert. The vegetation thins as the trail moves into the desert, which is not only drier, but also downwind of Halemaumau Crater whose sulfurous, choking fumes cause vegetation-killing acid rain.

The trail continues over 1982, 1971, and 1974 flows, and the Southwest Rift Zone, which is marked by large cracks and passes the start of the Kau Desert Trail. It reaches Jaggar Museum and then leads gently downhill along the edge of Uwekahuna Bluff. It passes Kilauea Military Camp shortly before reaching Steaming Bluff. Just after Steaming Bluff, the trail passes a turnoff to the Sulphur Bank Trail on the left and the Sandalwood Trail on the right. Go straight ahead to return to Volcano House.

"To Rest is Not to Conquer"

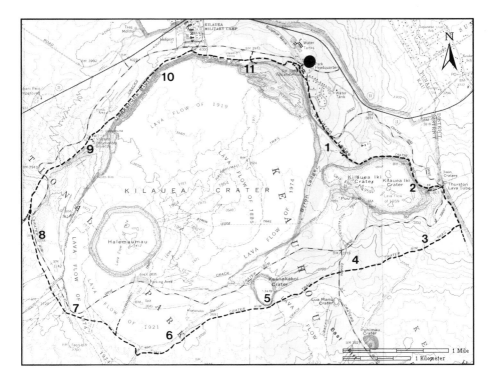

8. Kipuka Puaulu Trail (Bird Park)

Kilauea Summit
1 hour, loop trip
200 calories; easiest
1.2 miles, loop trip
Highest point: 4180 feet
Lowest point: 3940 feet
Map: Kilauea Crater 1:24,000
Hawaii Volcanoes National Park

A kipuka is an area of vegetation surrounded but not covered by lava flows. This island-like formation has taken on special importance since the arrival of the voracious cattle and goats brought by the Europeans. Rough lava flows surrounding kipukas may act as barriers to fire and to such all-devouring herbivores. Kipuka Puaulu is one such island of relatively unspoiled native Hawaiian forest. The National Park Service has done a commendable job of maintaining this loop trail, labelling plants, and eradicating the wild pigs which elsewhere do much damage tearing up the ground and spreading weed seeds.

The Kipuka Puaulu Trail, like others at higher elevations along the Puu Oo and Kaumana Trails (also described in this book), provides numerous examples of native Hawaiian plants and related animals. An excellent booklet written by the Hawaii Natural History Association describing the labelled plants on this self-guided trail may be purchased at Kilauea Visitor Center.

Route: From Kilauea Visitor Center drive out the park gate to Highway 11. Follow it left for 2.3 miles to Mauna Loa Road. Follow Mauna Loa Strip Road for 1.6 miles to the parking area next to the Kipuka Puaulu trailhead. The trailhead is marked by a display of some of the plants and birds you may see during this pleasant, easy hike.

Near the display, the trail passes through a fence designed to keep out wild pigs. The loop trail begins just beyond the fence. Take the left-hand fork around the loop's gentle course. The trail is nearly level, the route is obvious, and the path is well maintained. After 0.5 miles, a short side trail leads left to a remarkably large koa tree, about 50 yards off the trail.

Continue on the loop trail, passing large ohia trees along the way. Native Hawaiian birds may be seen in the nearby treetops. The most common is the apapane, a little, bright-red bird with black wings and tail. It is especially fond of the nectar of the red-blossomed ohia lehua trees. The iiwi, much rarer at this elevation, is colored like the apapane, but is somewhat larger and has a curved bill. These birds and others are best seen early in the morning or at evening, especially after a rain.

The loop ends at the gate. A short turn-off to the Kipuka Puaulu picnic area is a hundred yards toward Highway 11 on Mauna Loa Strip Road.

Kipuka Puaulu Trail

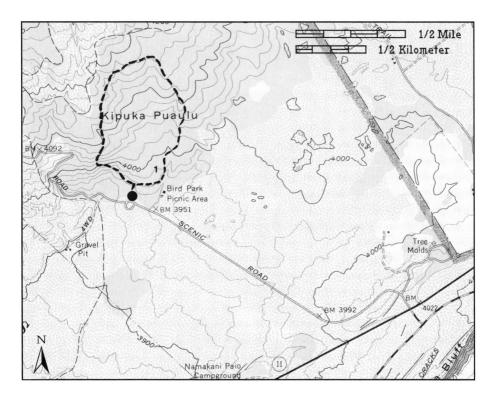

Southwest and East Rift Zones

The courses of the Southwest and the East Rift Zones of Kilauea Volcano are marked by craters, volcanic vents, and outpourings of lava. These rifts, which are areas of weakness in the rock, are miles long and deep. Magma forces its way up the rifts and spews out, forming volcanic cones and flooding the land with lava. In some places lava drains back down into the rifts or flows out lower down the rifts, causing the unsupported surface to collapse into large pit craters.

The Southwest Rift Zone runs from Kilauea Caldera through the Kau Desert and beyond it to the sea. The desert's length may be traversed by the 18.9-mile-long Kau Desert Trail and its width by the shorter Mauna Iki Trail. For an even shorter hike go only as far as the Footprints Exhibit or a mile beyond it to the black top of Mauna Iki Lava Shield. The Kau Desert Trail starts just southwest of Kilauea Caldera and ends at Hilina Pali Overlook on Hilina Pali Road. Kipuka Nene campground, a good place to spend the night, is along Hilina Pali Road.

As hikers in the strange Kau Desert will readily see, the earth is wedged open along the rifts, which causes the earthquakes common along the south coast of the island. The desert is covered with recent lava flows and ash, sprinkled with acid rain caused by fumes from eruptions, and is, thus, almost devoid of vegetation. Life here subsists sparsely and tenuously,

Volcanic Rift — Southwest Rift Zone

if at all, like the earth in some primordial geologic age. Yet, the evidences of the geologic forces at work lay bare and visible, in austere beauty, best seen in the long shadows of morning or after a rain shower brings out the blackness of the rocks.

The East Rift Zone, with deep craters and prominent cones producing ash and much lava, stretches generally east from Kilauea Caldera to Cape Kumukahi, the island's easternmost point. For its first three miles Chain of Craters Road follows the East Rift Zone. This section of the

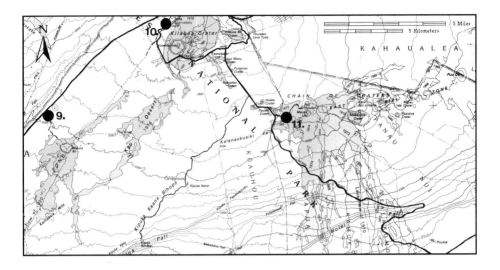

road threads southeast through verdant fern and ohia forest broken by deep craters and recent lava flows. Past Pauahi Crater the road reaches the abandoned course of Chain of Craters Road, now the turnoff to a viewpoint of Mauna Ulu, "growing mountain."

The Napau Crater Trail leads to the remarkable country beyond Mauna Ulu. It starts at the Mauna Ulu viewpoint and follows much of the course of the road obliterated by lava from 1969 to 1974. Because of the activity of nearby Puu Oo, permits for both hiking and wilderness camping are required. The volcanic vents upwind of the campsite can be troublesome neighbors. Night and day they may shower the site with ash and Pele's hair (threads of volcanic glass), billow out noxious fumes, and occasionally inundate nearby areas with molten lava.

Ohia Forest and Fresh Lava — East Rift Zone

9. Mauna Iki Trail

Southwest Rift Zone
10 hours, round trip
2100 calories; harder
17.6 miles, round trip
Highest point: 3200 feet
Lowest point: 2920 feet
Map: Kau Desert 1:24,000
Hawaii Volcanoes National Park

The Mauna Iki Trail traverses the Kau Desert from Highway 11 to Hilina Pali Road. The desert, covered by thin vegetation and small black ash dunes, takes on a stark beauty when shadows from a low morning sun show its textures. Lava flows, Pele's hair, deep cracks, craters, and wind-blown, jet-black ash create impressive scenes.

Hilina Pali Road, a possible pick-up site, is sometimes closed. Shorter round trip hikes to the Footprints Exhibit or Mauna Iki Lava Shield will still give good views of the desert.

Route: The trailhead is at a parking area and small photographic exhibit on Highway 11, nine miles southwest of Kilauea Visitor Center. At first the nearly level route follows an asphalt path over rough aa lava from Mauna Loa. It then comes to smooth pahoehoe lava from Kilauea. At 0.8 miles the trail reaches the Footprints Exhibit, which was built to display casts of footprints made in ash from the 1790 steam explosion of Kilauea Volcano and rediscovered in 1920.

In 1790 Kamehameha and his fierce cousin, Keoua, were at war. As the army of Keoua retreated south through the Kau Desert, the unusual steam eruption killed many of his warriors and their families. Viewed as a sign of Pele's displeasure, it demoralized Keoua and hastened his ultimate defeat.

During the eruption small particles of

Dunes — East Kau Desert

roasted volcanic material dampened by steam fell to the ground. Running people left their footprints in this cement. The sun dried the cement. A second layer of cement shrouded and preserved the scene.

After the exhibit the trail continues toward Mauna Iki, the low, black, lava dome created in the eruptions of 1919-20. Wind-blown, black ash and outcrops of pahoehoe, in a vast array of shapes, form the landscape. Winds in the area are sometimes laden with fumes. The trail meets the Kau Desert Trail at the low top of Mauna Iki.

Footprints Exhibit

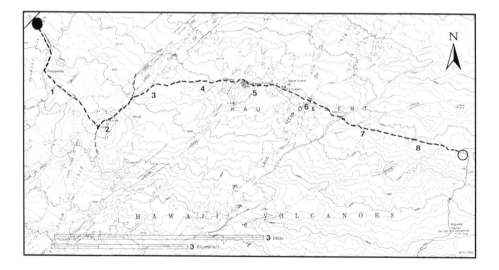

To continue across the desert follow the Kau Desert Trail north for 0.7 miles to a turnoff on the right, a continuation of the Mauna Iki Trail. This reaches Hilina Pali Road in 6.3 more miles. Along the way the trail passes Puu Koae spatter cone, lava flows from 1974, and the steep-walled Twin Pit Craters. Ahu in open terrain mark the route.

10. Kau Desert Trail
Southwest Rift Zone

1-2 days, one way
10 hours, one way
2200 calories; hardest
18.9 miles, one way
Highest point: 3930 feet
Lowest point: 1700 feet
Maps: Kilauea Crater, Kau Desert, Wood Valley 1:24,000
Hawaii Volcanoes National Park

The Kau Desert has sufficient rain for plants to grow; however, lava flows, black volcanic ash, and Pele's hair repeatedly cover it. Those few plants that might grow between times of volcanic activity are thoroughly discouraged by the acid rain and fumes swept down from Kilauea Caldera by the strong northeast trade winds.

The long Kau Desert Trail starts just southwest of Kilauea Caldera and ends at Hilina Pali Overlook on Hilina Pali Road. A ride from there will spare hikers from facing a dusty wind in an uphill return suitable only for troubled souls doing penance for past sins. The descent from Kilauea Caldera to the Pepeiao Cabin is steady downhill with the gritty wind, mercifully, at one's back. Intricate lava formations, rifts, and fractures, volcanic cones and craters, and a short walk up Mauna Iki Lava Shield add interest. In such a desert there is solitude; the scenes, so unlike elsewhere, are close to the realms of imagination.

Obtain an overnight backcountry permit at Kilauea Visitor Center. Check in upon return, (808) 967-7311. Discuss your plans with the rangers and find out about cabin use and water supply (treat it). Carry a good supply of water and a tent. If the volcano is too active or your respiratory system is susceptible, skip this trip.

Route: Take Crater Rim Drive from Kilauea Visitor Center for 2.7 miles to

"Shark Tooth" Lava

Hawaiian Volcano Observatory and the Jaggar Museum. Start on the Crater Rim Trail at the south end of the parking lot and follow it south for about a mile. The trail crosses Crater Rim Drive along the way before it reaches the Kau Desert Trail leading off, southwest, into the Kau Desert.

The landscape of ohelo bushes and stunted ohia trees at the trailhead soon changes to nearly barren pahoehoe lava as the trail enters the desert. The older lava, often covered by wind-borne ash makes

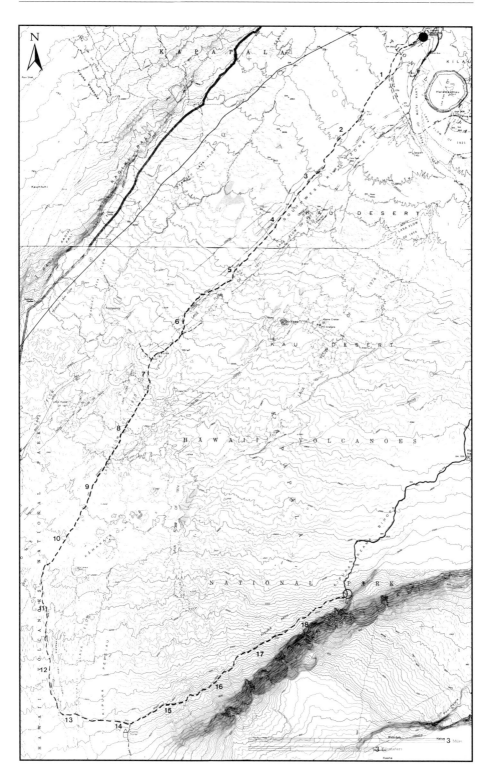

Along the Trail from Pepeiao Cabin

End of the Trail at Hilina Pali Road

easy walking. Cross rifts and cracks along the route with caution.

The trail descends gently. At 6.1 miles from the parking lot it passes a turnoff to the Mauna Iki Trail extension on the left (east). At 0.7 more miles the beginning part of the Mauna Iki Trail comes in from the right, from the Footprints Shelter and Highway 11. At the same time, the trail reaches the top of Mauna Iki, a broad, low lava shield cone. Continue straight on.

Mauna Iki continues to smolder malevolently since its eruption in 1919-20, which left small craters at its top. Stay on the trail. The pahoehoe lava is weak or hollow in places and can suddenly collapse.

After about two and a half miles the trail passes by the Kamakaia Hills, small, rounded cones of bare lava. Beyond them the trail swings east and passes over expanses of rough aa lava and wind-blown ash. Then small ohia trees and grassy flats appear, a much appreciated return of kindred life after the long desolation of lava. About 4 miles past the Kamakaia Hills and 7.3 miles from the top of Mauna Iki, the trail comes out of the desert and reaches a short spur to Pepeiao Cabin and campsite. The cabin has three bunks and a rain catchment tank.

From the spur, the trail climbs gradually for 4.8 miles, northeast, to the end of Hilina Pali Road, the trail's terminus. Kipukas along the way, now mostly covered by grassland and charred stumps, not long ago supported native forest. The alien broomsedge, which has spread into the area, uses fire to wrest the sun for itself. The park suppressed the goats which once plagued the forests, but the broomsedge now builds up a heavy load of dead straw. This burns hotly, killing the shady trees, but not its own safely buried roots.

11. Napau Crater Trail
East Rift Zone

7 hours, round trip
1800 calories; harder
14 miles, round trip
Highest point: 3440 feet
Lowest point: 2700 feet
Maps: Volcano, Makaopuhi 1:24,000
Hawaii Volcanoes National Park

Mauna Ulu grew in 1969 out of the recesses of the ohia forest, with spectacular fountains and repeated flows of lava. Chain of Craters Road was rerouted further to the west, away from the flows of lava. The Napau Crater Trail follows the approximate course of the old road to Makaopuhi Crater. The trail then continues to its end at Napau Crater and a good view of the new volcanic cone, Puu Oo, built by eruptions in the 1980's and 1990's.

Check at Kilauea Visitor Center about volcanic activity in the area and for travel limitations and safety information. Register for hiking and camping. If the volcano is erupting, the area may be affected by fumes, pumice, cinders, and Pele's hair. The waterless, primitive campsite at the end of the trail is downwind of volcanic vents and particularly susceptible to fallout from them.

Route: From Kilauea Visitor Center take Crater Rim Drive for 3 miles to Chain of Craters Road. Drive for 3.5 miles south on Chain of Craters Road, to just past Pauahi Crater. Take the turnoff, east, to the viewpoint of Mauna Ulu. The trail leads northeast from the end of the turnoff.

The trail at first goes a short distance through returning vegetation and then across fresher flows of pahoehoe lava from Mauna Ulu. At 1.2 miles it reaches Puu Huluhulu and a short spur trail to the viewpoint at its top. This small cinder cone is an island of greenery in the expanse of lava. The small crater at its top is filled with a flourishing native ohia forest protected from lava and wild pigs. This is a good turning point for a shorter hike.

The pahoehoe-covered trail continues, northeast, over the low pass between Puu Huluhulu and glowering Mauna Ulu, 2,000 yards to the south. As the trail swings around Mauna Ulu Lava Shield it passes lava channels, collapsed areas, and pahoehoe in a great variety of shapes. From the northeast side of Mauna Ulu the trail swings southerly to gradually ascend the Alae Shield, which was a deep crater before Mauna Ulu's eruption.

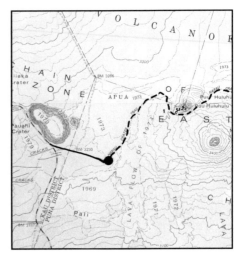

The trail turns east, reaching Makaopuhi Crater at four miles, where it leaves the barren flows of 1970's lava to enter thin ohia forest on the south side of the crater. It then joins the course of a nineteenth century single lane road. After another half a mile it passes by a turnoff to the Kalapana Trail and the Naulu Trail leading to Chain of Craters Road in about three miles.

The Napau Crater Trail continues east, hugging the south side of Makaopuhi Crater. It enters a thick forest of tree ferns and ohia and at 1.5 miles from the junction it reaches the stone ruins of the "pulu factory," once a collection point for pulu from tree ferns.

Tree Molds and Puu Oo Vent

At 0.5 miles past the pulu factory a spur trail branches left to the primitive camping area, flanked on the north by 1960's lava flows and a lava cast forest. Fuming Puu Oo is visible two miles to the southeast. The main trail passes by this spur and continues east across an 1840 lava flow to end soon at the edge of Napau Crater. Because of volcanic hazards the area past Napau Crater may be closed. Return as you came.

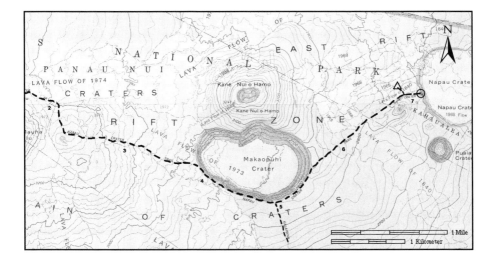

Coastal Region

Great terraces and pali slopes, draped by shiny pahoehoe or dull aa lava, evidence the downward faulting along the south side of Kilauea Volcano. The flat, lava-filled terraces and the coastal plains are created when lava, flowing from the rift zones above, fills low areas formed by the faults. Low cliffs meet the rough sea, making this coast unsuited for swimming.

These unpopulated lava fields, hot and parched much of the year, can also display the green of new growth where soils have formed on older flows. When higher or windward regions on the island are wet or cool, here it may remain balmy and dry.

Chain of Craters Road leads down to the coast, where lava flows blocked it in the 1980's and 1990's. Along the road there is no access to fuel, food, water, or telephones. High on the pali, Kealakomo Overlook offers a grand vista to the Puna Coast and distant Kau; a landscape of lava, pali, and ocean, crossed by unfrequented trails to the remote seashore oases of Keauhou, Halape, and Kaaha.

The remnants of man's activities may be preserved by the dry climate and the watchful personnel of the park, but nothing can be saved from the invading lava. The village sites at Kealakomo, Laeapuki, and Kamoamoa, as well as the delightful nearby campground, have become but names and fading memories. Wahaula Heiau, the ancient Hawaiian temple, is surrounded by fresh lava. Protruding from the lava, are heat-twisted steel girders, all that is left of the park's Wahaula Visitor Center.

What remains is, perhaps, the best collection of petroglyphs in the Hawaiian Islands. The short Puuloa Petroglyphs Trail, off Chain of Craters Road, takes you there. The rock carvings show men and women, animals, boats, and forms not yet deciphered. The long Puna Coast Trail is for the more adventuresome. It follows a flat course across the hot, barren lava plain to the campsites at Keauhou and Halape.

At the end of Chain of Craters Road, the park service may mark out a trail by which visitors can approach the scene of flowing lava in relative safety. At Pele's whim, rivers of lava stream down the pali and into the

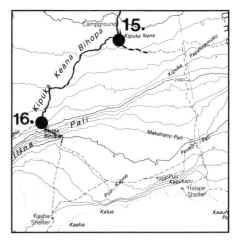

ocean, clouds of vapor rise from the boiling sea, great sections of lava drop into the sea with deadly suddenness, and new black sand beaches are formed.

The Halape and Kaaha Trails can be reached from Hilina Pali Road, the only offshoot from Chain of Crater Road. This road is sometimes closed because of fire danger. The trailhead of the Halape Trail is at Kipuka Nene Campground, five miles down the road, in grassland scattered with scorched trees. The campground has a picnic pavilion, pit toilets, a fireplace, and a water catchment tank (treatment needed). Small plants, sensitive to the touch, grow nearby. Nene geese quietly drop in to pay their respects to their new neighbors. Do not feed them, since it will only do them harm.

As with the other campsites in the coastal region, sleeping accommodations are the bare, hard rock, the domain of various tiny creatures earnestly seeking an honest meal. Bring ground pads and insect-proof, free-standing tents. Slumbering campers will feel the slight trembles of the earth as Pele wanders her dark land.

Hilina Pali Road continues to descend gradually for four more miles through the sparse forest between the Kau Desert and the coastal pali. It ends at Kipuka Keana

Wahaulu Heiau Site

Bihopa and the windswept overlook at the rim of Hilina Pali, the most prominent of the region's fault scarps. A picnic pavilion displays a picture exhibit. The route to the Kaaha Shelter and campsite on the coast starts here on the Hilina Pali Trail and then joins the Kaaha Trail. This is also the end of the long Kau Desert Trail coming in from Pepeiao Cabin and campsite.

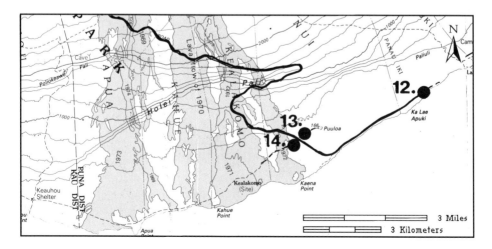

12. Active Lava Flows
Coastal Region
2-3 hours, round trip
300-500 calories; easier
1-2 miles, round trip
Highest Point: sea level
Lowest Point: sea level
Maps: Makaopuhi Crater, Kalapana 1:24,000
Hawaii Volcanoes National Park

The chance of seeing a volcano in action is one of the attractions of Hawaii Volcanoes National Park. During recent years the vents have been centered on the East Rift Zone, beyond Napau Crater, in areas far removed from roads. Flows produced from the East Rift Zone have streamed down the pali to the coastal plain and the ocean, forming lava tubes and channels, and crossing the coastal road that once lead to Kalapana. The coastal plain has, in recent years, been the most accessible area for viewing lava flows. The nearest road access to them has been by Chain of Craters Road, a 50-mile round trip from Kilauea Visitor Center.

Hawaii's basaltic magma has less entrapped gas and is richer in metals than the glassy magma in volcanoes like Mt. St. Helens. Because of this, Hawaii's lava is less viscous and forms into long streams of smooth pahoehoe lava and then, as it cools and loses gas, into rough aa lava. Hawaii's volcanoes are built up by layer upon layer of long, thin lava flows spreading over broad, gentle slopes. At vents, cones are built, such as, steep-sided Puu Oo cone on the East Rift Zone.

The park, with knowledge born of sad experience, closes the areas around volcanic vents to travel. Other areas may be open only during certain daylight hours. Volcanic activity changes from year to year and even from moment to moment. Thus, any specific description of a trail

End of Chain of Craters Road

marked by the park to viewing places would soon be obsolete. Obtain information and publications from Kilauea Visitor Center regarding the current trail and viewing area. Call (808) 967-7977 for the latest eruption activity.

Route: To reach the coastal area where flows or clouds of water vapor from lava entering the sea might be seen, drive from Kilauea Visitor Center south on Crater Rim Drive for 3 miles to Chain of Craters Road. Follow the road for over 20 miles

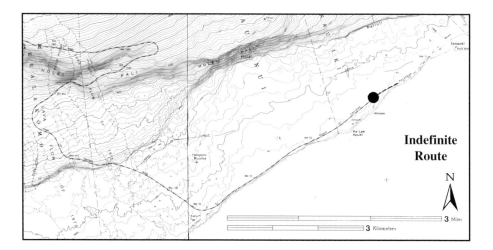

down to its end at the coast. There is no gas, food, water, or telephone along Chain of Craters Road. Cut in the 1970's by lava from the Mauna Ulu eruption, it was rerouted and rebuilt, but to no avail. Lava flows streaming down from the East Rift Zone of Kilauea in the 1980's and 1990's have blocked it at the coast.

The Park's Visitor Center and the ancient Wahaula Heiau were inundated by lava in 1989. Nothing is left of the center but twisted steel girders. The nearby, delightful site of Kamoamoa Village and campground met a like fate in 1993, as did Laeapuki Village.

From the end of the road one may be able to follow a current marked trail as far as common sense and park warning signs permit. Any route will be dictated by current safety considerations. Follow the park service markers and instructions and STAY ON THE TRAIL. Some dangers are not apparent.

Occasionally, flowing lava may be seen, but usually it is contained within lava tubes. Lava flows produce steam explosions, dangerous fumes, and acid rain as they hit the ocean. Great clouds of water vapor billow up. Lava fragments build black-sand beaches down-current of the flows. The fumes of hydrochloric acid and

Wahaula Vistor Center

sulfur compounds make the area unsuited for children and those with lung or heart problems. Near the shore, great sections of land may suddenly collapse into the ocean, and have done so with loss of life. The fresh lava may collapse underfoot.

The coastal area is hot and the fresh black lava collects the sun's heat. Bring sunglasses, water, and protection from the sun.

13. Puuloa Petroglyphs Trail
Coastal Region
1 hour, round trip
200 calories; easiest
1.4 miles, round trip
Highest point: 166 feet
Lowest point: 125 feet
Maps: Makaopuhi Crater, Kalapana 1:24,000
Hawaii Volcanoes National Park

The coastal lava plain of Kilauea was long populated by the Hawaiians, but volcanism is steadily erasing the evidences of their presence. The stone ruins of Wahaula Heiau and the villages sites of Laeapuki and Kamoamoa along the coastal section of Chain of Craters Road were once places of great interest. The village sites, the heiau, and the Kamoamoa camping area were inundated by lava flows in 1993 and earlier.

Yet, the Puna Coast remains perhaps the best place for viewing petroglyphs in all the Hawaiian Islands. The fresh lava along this coast was a particularly good surface for rock artists. The dry weather preserves the petroglyphs and limits the growth of vegetation. The Puuloa Petroglyphs Trail off Chain of Craters Road has a fine collection of such petroglyphs.

Sites for petroglyphs were not chosen at random. What made this site so favored is as puzzling as is its name, "Puuloa." Puuloa means "long hill," which is an odd name for such a small geographic feature. Perhaps there is some connection with the greatest geological feature of the Hawaiian Islands, Mauna Loa, which means "long mountain." Perhaps Puuloa's orientation to the night sky provides some clue.

Route: From Kilauea Visitor Center go south on Crater Rim Drive for 3 miles to its intersection with Chain of Craters Road, which leads down to the coast. Follow Chain of Craters Road for 16.5 miles, until it reaches the flat coastal lava plain at the foot of the pali. The trailhead, marked with interpretive signs, is on the left side of the road, across from the Puna Coast Trail trailhead on the right side. The easy trail leads in a generally straight line northeast until it reaches a boardwalk constructed by the park service for viewing the petroglyphs.

Pictures of people, boats, sails, and other objects may be seen from the boardwalk. A common pattern is circles. It is said that umbilical cords were left in these. There are some curious carvings which look almost like Arabic script.

Photography is best at Puuloa when the sun is low, either shortly after sunrise or before sunset. In the middle of the day the sun heats the lava rocks unpleasantly and the light is too flat to show the petroglyphs to advantage. A telephoto lens is handy for taking undistorted photos from the boardwalk surrounding the petroglyphs.

Petroglyphs

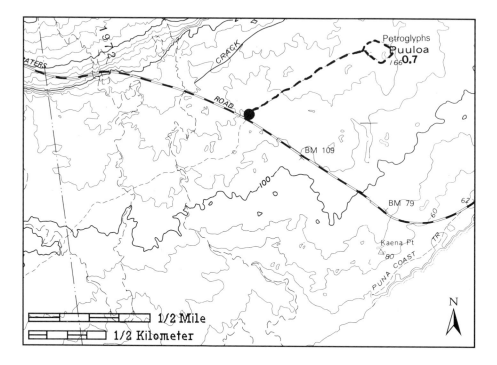

14. Puna Coast Trail
Coastal Region

2 days, round trip
14 hours, round trip
2800 calories; hardest
22.6 miles, round trip
Highest point: 150 feet
Lowest point: sea level
Maps: Makaopuhi Crater, Kau Desert 1:24,000
Hawaii Volcanoes National Park

The heat of the tropical sun on the shadeless Puna Coast is absorbed by the black lava plain and radiates upward leaving the traveller like an insect trapped atop a warming griddle. Still, a hiker, understanding man's scant claim to authority over this place, may, with cunning timing, cross it to good advantage. The reward at the end of this long, flat trail is Halape, an isolated oasis and shallow green lagoon of austere beauty.

First, get up-to-date information and register for back-country travel at Kilauea Visitor Center. Pack plenty of water, have good sun protection, and carry a ground pad and an insect proof, free standing tent. Begin the hike not later than at the first light of dawn and do not return in the afternoon. Midday already is far too hot for travel on the black lava, which emits heat collected from the sun well into evening's darkness. Consider a hike in combination with the Halape Trail.

Route: From Kilauea Visitor Center take Crater Rim Drive for 3 miles to Chain of Craters Road. Follow it about 16.5 miles to the coastal lava plain. The signed trailhead for the Puna Coast Trail is on the right side of the road, across from the trailhead to the Puuloa Petroglyphs Trail.

The flat route is easy to follow, as is the path to hell. Keep the ocean on the left and follow the ahu (stone cairns). The view is unbroken from water's edge to far up the rounded pali. The smooth trail crosses the bare 1960's and 1970's pahoehoe or aa lava. Access to the cooling ocean is blocked by low, recently formed sea cliffs in all but a few places, such as, at sparsely vegetated, windswept Apua Point, 6.6 miles along the trail. Nowhere is it safe to swim.

At 9.7 miles the trail reaches Keauhou Landing, once used for pulu and cattle shipment. It is the end of the rough and rarely used Keauhou Trail, which starts high up on Chain of Craters Road. The nearby Keauhou Shelter may have water in its tank (needs treatment). West of the landing the path leads up a fault between earthquake-shifted blocks. From the top of this climb Halape can be seen, marked by an offshore islet close to the foot of the prominence, Puu Kapukapu.

Continue for 1.6 miles to reach Halape,

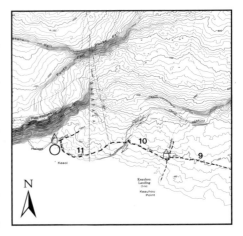

Puna Coast — Halape in the Distance

the terminus of the trail. The primitive three-walled shelter, prudently situated uphill from tsunami (tidal waves), has a tank which may have water (treat it). A crack near the shore has brackish, possibly contaminated water. Palm trees, thoughtfully planted by park rangers, thrive inland of the green lagoon, the site of the coconut grove inundated when the coast dropped in the earthquake and tsunami of 1975. Campsites are east of the beach.

Be considerate of sea turtles, an ancient and endangered species, which lay their eggs here. Read the park's brochure on turtles and heed the signs. Do not build campfires on the beaches or leave food to attract mongooses and feral cats, which prey on baby turtles. In spring and summer view the Milky Way and stars of the Southern Hemisphere: our neighbor, brilliant Alpha Centauri, the southern cross, and the great constellation Scorpio with its red giant, Antares. If you feel a strong earthquake, run uphill immediately to avoid multiple tsunami.

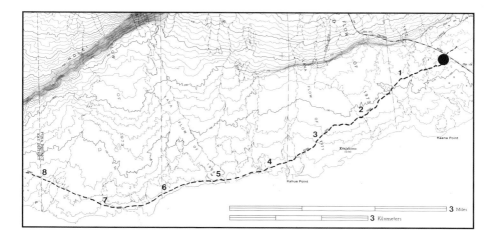

15. Halape Trail

Coastal Region

1-2 days, round trip
4 hours down; 6 hours up
3000 calories; hardest
14.4 miles, round trip
Highest point: 2925 feet
Lowest point: sea level
Maps: Makaopuhi Crater, Kau Desert 1:24,000
Hawaii Volcanoes National Park

The wilderness campsite at the coastal oasis of Halape, on the hot, dry, south Kau Coast is reached only by long, barren trails. Halape's green cove and small, white coral beach are rarities on this desolate coast. A replanted grove of coconut trees at Halape taps the underground fresh water which floats on the ocean water underlying the coast.

The earthquake of November 1975, which was accompanied by huge, deadly tsunami, wiped out old Halape. In the scale of geologic time, such waves occur often along this coast. This side of the island periodically drops and moves outward at fault lines visible inland. Even larger waves and earthquakes have caused massive destruction along this coast, as in 1868. If you feel a large earthquake here, run uphill immediately.

Register at Kilauea Visitor Center for wilderness camping, obtain the brochures on the coastal areas and turtles, and make sure that Hilina Pali Road is not closed because of fire danger. Carry a ground pad and an insect proof, free-standing tent.

Route: From Kilauea Visitor Center drive south on Crater Rim Drive for 3 miles around Kilauea Iki Crater to Chain of Craters Road. Follow Chain of Craters Road south for 2.3 miles to its junction with Hilina Pali Road. Continue on Hilina Pali Road for 5.0 miles to Kipuka Nene Campground and picnic area.

Kipuka Nene has pit toilets, a picnic

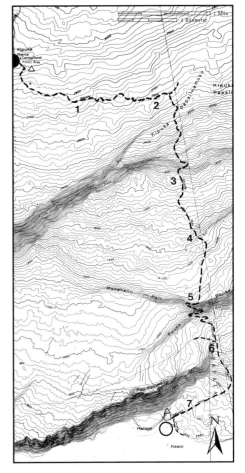

pavilion and a water tank which, usually, has water (treat it). The trail starts at the back of the pavilion and heads south on an abandoned dirt road. The trail goes through sparse forest and grassland for over two

The Earthquake's Creation — Halape

miles. It then turns south toward the ocean, leaves the main dirt road, and soon changes into a steep trail down rocky lava flows.

At 5.6 miles the Hilina Pali Trail comes in from the west near Puu Kapukapu, a hillock to the southwest. Past this junction descend for 1.6 miles to reach Halape and its small crescent-shaped, white coral beach. If wading be careful not to step on sea urchins. Among the breakers lies the site of the idyllic grove of coconut trees that once graced Halape. Be careful not to interfere with sea turtles which may lay their eggs around the beach. Lights or fires confuse them and food left out attracts predators.

The shelter has been prudently situated well inland to protect it from the infrequent but inevitable tsunami waves. The campsites are east of the beach and cove. There is brackish water in a large crack 75 yards directly inland from the beach. Use care to keep it free of soap and sun screen.

Water may be available from the tank at the shelter (treat it). Use a tent to avoid the unpleasantness of night roaming centipedes, scorpions, and the like. The shadeless uphill return to Kipuka Nene can be hot. It is best hiked early in the morning.

16. Kaaha Trail via Hilina Pali
Coastal Region
1-2 days, round trip
3 hours down; 4 hours up
1300 calories; harder
7.6 miles, round trip
Highest point: 2280 feet
Lowest point: sea level
Map: Kau Desert 1:24,000
Hawaii Volcanoes National Park

On the barren coast of Kau, the hiker feels insignificant in the scale of the surroundings. Here, one may view the blue of the sky and the broad, lonely landscape, set against the ocean's immensity. As far as the eye may see, there are desolate fields of lava welled up from far below. The broad ocean, rolling in free from Antarctica, tears at the shore.

Once, long ago, Hawaiian fishermen, drawn by the fresh water found in cracks near Kaaha, were content to call this home, apparently happy in simplicity. Now, there is the wind, the rock, the sea, and the grass. Along the shore morning glory, with its deep roots tapping the fresh water floating on the salt, adds welcome touches of green foliage and pretty blue and white flowers.

Register at Kilauea Visitor Center for overnight travel and current information. Check to see that the road is not closed because of fire danger. Take along extra water and be prepared to treat the water, if available, at the shelter catchment tank. Have long pants for travel through heavy grass, a shady hat, a ground pad, and a free standing, insect proof tent.

Route: From Kilauea Visitor Center drive south for 3 miles to Chain of Craters Road, which descends toward the ocean. Follow it for 2.3 miles to a turnoff on the right onto Hilina Pali Road. Follow that narrow, paved road for 9 miles to its end at Hilina Pali Lookout, a shelter with a pho-

Kaaha Shelter

tographic display and a waterless, small picnic area. The lookout is also the end of the Kau Desert Trail coming in from Pepeiao Cabin.

From the lookout, the route to Kaaha Shelter goes south down the Hilina Pali Trail, with switchbacks dug well into the pali. Shortly after reaching a sloping grassy plain, the trail reaches the start of the Kaaha Trail, leading off to the right. Carefully follow the ahu (stone cairns), as the trail may have rough footing and may be obscured and obstructed by heavy grass.

After crossing the grassy plain the trail nears a second pali and passes another difficult to find turnoff toward Puu Kapukapu and Halape. The trail then descends more steeply down the small pali above Kaaha Shelter. Recent cracks in the barren lava give evidence of the earthquakes repeatedly felt along this coast as it slumps into the ocean along the fault lines formed at the pali.

Cooling off in Kaaha

The shelter, visible at the base of the lower pali, was built prudently upland out of the reach of the massive tidal waves which immediately follow earthquakes along this coast. There is no beach, but what sea cliffs may have formed have sunken in the earthquakes. The sea laps inland in many rocky pools.

About 3 miles southeast from the shelter along the shore is the rootless cone, Na Puu o na Elemakule. It was formed when an ancient lava flow hit the ocean, tossing up debris along the edge of the shore. From there a little used route climbs inland to Pepeiao Cabin.

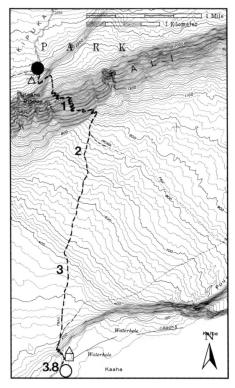

Mauna Loa Climbs

Mauna Loa's volume is enormous — about 10,000 cubic miles in all. From the ocean floor, this gently sloping shield volcano rises approximately 30,000 feet to its summit, making this formation taller than Mt. Everest and far more massive.

The trails on Mauna Loa are in a class by themselves in Hawaiian hiking. They require almost no scrambling, but because of length, altitude, and weather, these hikes must be treated as climbs. Only strong, experienced hikers should attempt either route.

Long is the best word to describe the climb up the Mauna Loa Trail. It is physically exhausting and most memorable. The trailhead is reached by taking Highway 11 in Hawaii Volcanoes National Park to Mauna Loa Strip Road and following it up for 13.5 miles to 6,662 feet. Puu Ulaula (Red Hill) Cabin is 7.5 miles up the trail at 10,035 feet, the first night's stop. From here the trail climbs the northeast rift.

The Observatory Trail is a somewhat shorter trek and is approached from the north side of Mauna Loa. It starts high, at the elevation of 11,000 feet, and is two hours away from Kilauea Visitor Center via Hilo and the Saddle Road.

Both of the trails meet at the rim of Mokuaweoweo Caldera. From there the Cabin Trail continues on to Mauna Loa Cabin at 13,250 feet. This is the terminus for both routes and can serve as a base for those wishing to proceed back around the

Morning Climb

west side of the caldera to the true summit of Mauna Loa. To reach the summit, follow the signed trail, marked with ahu, along the west rim of the caldera. At these altitudes the more than 9-mile round trip to the summit and back to the cabin should be considered an all-day affair.

Equipment and Planning

In planning the climb, check with the park rangers for current information, safety factors, and advice regarding the suitability of your equipment. The trailheads are many miles from the main roads, with neither water nor phones. There is little hope of hitching rides.

Overnight hikers must register at Kilauea Visitor Center in Hawaii Volcanoes National Park for backcountry permits and the use of the two cabins on the mountain. Kilauea Visitor Center is open daily from 7:45 to 4:45, telephone (808) 967-7311. Permits are issued no earlier than noon of the day before the hike on a first-come

Mauna Loa — The Great Shield Volcano Viewed from Mauna Kea

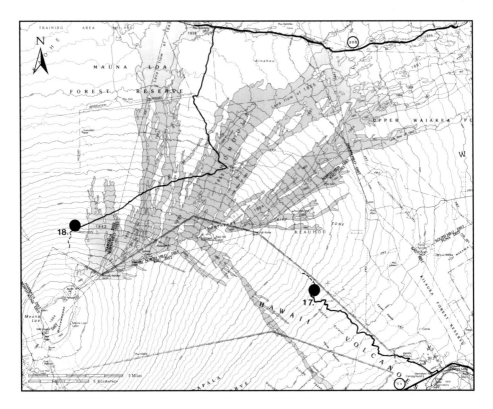

Which Way Next?

basis. Groups are limited to 12 persons and stays up to 3 nights per cabin. Check on the level of catchment water at the cabins. Puu Ulaula (Red Hill) Cabin has 8 bunks with mattresses. Mauna Loa Cabin, the terminus of both routes, has 12 bunks with mattresses. Apart from the cabin tanks, water may be available from ice in a crack south of Mauna Loa Cabin and sometimes in other cracks or from snow along the trail.

The careful climber will include plenty of heavy wool or polypropylene clothing and a warm sleeping bag in a plastic stuff bag, rain gear, dark goggles for snow, sunblock, warm and shady hat, ample water, water treatment material, food, flashlight with extra batteries and bulb, topographical maps, compass, altimeter, tent, first aid kit, mirror, and cooking and eating gear, most of which items are considered essentials by the park. Be sure to wear heavy, well broken-in boots and allow enough time.

Precautions

Snow, extreme cold, fog, high winds, and cold rain can occur at any time of year on Mauna Loa. Weather may be cloudy for days at a time and the trail and its ahu (stone cairns) may be obscured by snow which may also form weak cornices and hide dropoffs. In bad weather call off the trip—the mountain will still be there.

You will not be lost as long as you know where you came from. The park will initiate a search 24 hours after they are notified by your friends that you are lost. Bright or reflective materials by day and flashlights at night (flashed in distress signals of three) may help in such cases.

Beware of sunburn and snow blindness. Sunlight is much stronger here than at lower elevations since there is less atmosphere above to filter out ultraviolet light or deflect the sun's rays. The days are long, the sun is high, and the snow is clean. Eyes need to be protected by dark goggles. Sunblock must

South across Mokuaweoweo Caldera

be used, but clothing is still the best protection. Words are seldom enough to impress those who have never been sunburned in the mountains. Experience is an effective teacher, but a cruel one.

Headaches, pounding heart, nausea, lethargy, and rapid breathing are indications of the effects of altitude and may be symptoms of mountain or altitude sickness. It affects some people and not oth-ers. It is always unpleasant and can even be fatal. The only immediate cure is descent. Prescription medicines taken a few days prior to climbing can help.

17. Mauna Loa via Red Hill
Mauna Loa Climbs

3-4 days, round trip
13-18 hours up; 10-15 hours down
8700 calories; hardest
38.2 miles, round trip
Highest point: 13,250 feet
Lowest point: 6,662 feet
Maps: Kipuka Pakekake, Kokoolau, Mauna Loa, Puu Ulaula 1:24,000
Hawaii Volcanoes National Park

It is said of Mount Fuji, "He who does not climb Fuji once is a fool; he who climbs it twice is also a fool." Some would say the same of Mauna Loa. However, the written word cannot express the experience of hiking along the great northeast rift of Mauna Loa, past mile upon mile of iridescent lava. Nor can words express the beauty of the transparent night sky at the summit, stretching to both hemispheres, or of the dawn light creeping across huge Mokuaweoweo Caldera, a great lake-like expanse of still cooling lava. Not a living thing is in view. The air is cold and rare.

Distances, altitude, volcanism, and Arctic weather dictate that this be considered a mountain climb for only the experienced and well-equipped. Read "Mauna Loa Climbs" description for necessary considerations. You must register for the climb at Kilauea Visitor Center. Check with the rangers about safety, current information, water supply, and the suitability of your

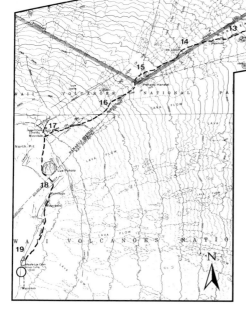

clothing and equipment. Find out about the use of Puu Ulaula (Red Hill) Cabin at 10,035 feet and Mauna Loa Cabin at 13,250 feet. Both cabins have mattresses, bunks, and water catchment tanks.

Route: From Kilauea Visitor Center go west on Highway 11 about 2.3 miles to follow little-used Mauna Loa Strip Road for 13.5 miles to its end at the 6,662-foot level. The trailhead is at the waterless lookout and parking area at the road's end. The trail contours easterly and then passes uphill through a goat gate.

The trail ascends through steadily diminishing vegetation to the Northeast Rift Zone with its line of volcanic vents, ash, and lava. At 7.5 miles and 4-6 hours from the start, the trail reaches Puu Ulaula (Red Hill) Cabin. From this first night's resting place, the trail climbs a barren route along the Northeast Rift Zone over lava flows with rock formations of bizarre shapes and colors, past spatter cones, and across large volcanic cracks. The route may change because of new lava, but will probably be marked by ahu (stone cairns).

At 17 miles from the start or 9.5 miles from Red Hill Cabin, the trail reaches a double intersection of trails on the northeast rim of North Pit, the northern "bay" of great Mokuaweoweo Caldera. The Observatory Trail comes up from the right. The Summit Trail leads right to par-

Mauna Loa Lava River

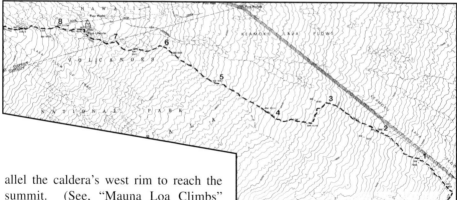

allel the caldera's west rim to reach the summit. (See, "Mauna Loa Climbs" description and "the Observatory Trail" map). The Cabin Trail leads to the end of this route and the second night's resting place at Mauna Loa Cabin.

The route to the cabin goes southerly across smooth lava in North Pit. It skirts the fragile southwest rim of Lua Poholo, a deep secondary crater with no warning of its edge, in poor visibility, a fatal drop-off. Beyond Lua Poholo, the trail climbs generally south to Mokuaweoweo Caldera's east rim. It reaches Mauna Loa Cabin at the 13,250-foot level after about 11.6 miles and 9-12 hours from Red Hill Cabin.

18. Mauna Loa via the Observatory Trail

Mauna Loa Climbs

1-2 days, round trip
5-6 hours up; 4-5 hours down
3500 calories; hardest
12 miles, round trip
Highest point: 13,250 feet
Lowest point: 11,060 feet
Maps: Kokoolau, Mauna Loa, 1:24,000
Hawaii Volcanoes National Park

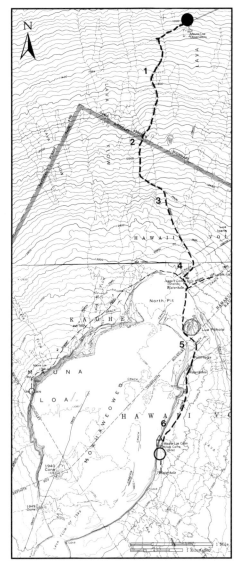

The physical effort involved to complete this route is only slightly less than that required for the Red Hill route. The rapid gain to high elevation may make altitude sickness more likely on this route. Climbers must be prepared for high winds, trail obscuring fog, and wet or freezing conditions. Read, "Mauna Loa Climbs" description for necessary considerations.

You must register at Kilauea Visitor Center in Hawaii Volcanoes National Park, a two-hour drive away from the trailhead, telephone (808) 967-7311. Check with park rangers regarding safety factors, current information, water supply, the suitability of your clothing and equipment, use of the cabin, and to see if the Observatory Road is open.

Start walking at or before first light. No water is available at the trailhead or along the trail. Allow plenty of time and be sure to inform the rangers after you get back.

Route: Take Highway 200 (Saddle Road) to near the crest of the saddle between Mauna Kea and Mauna Loa, about 27 miles from Hilo. Just before reaching Puu Huluhulu, a small but prominent wooded cone in a sea of bare lava, a paved road leads to the left. Follow this road about 18 miles until the Mauna Loa Weather Observatory at 11,000 feet elevation comes into view.

Park about 300 yards below the Observatory, where a jeep road leads off to the right. Walk the jeep road for about

June on Mauna Loa

800 yards to the signed trailhead. Follow the ahu (rock cairns), which lead directly up the mountain on flows of smooth pahoehoe lava. You will also encounter rough aa lava. After about two miles the trail veers left, joining a jeep road. After passing a gate the trail leaves the road to continue up more directly, over ash and pahoehoe lava flows. It eventually recrosses the road.

The trail is marked by ahu. Do not lose sight of them. If you do, return to the last one you saw and start again. Snow usually covers the upper regions during winter and early spring. Depending on snow level the ahu may either be covered or stand out against the white snow.

After a long climb of 3-4 hours the trail levels out and reaches the northeast rim of Mokuaweoweo Caldera, where it meets the Mauna Loa Trail coming up from the left. At this double junction, the Summit Trail leads west (right) up to the summit. The route to the terminus of the trail at Mauna Loa Cabin continues on the Cabin Trail.

Take the Cabin Trail by following ahu southerly across the smooth floor of North Pit, skirting the southwest rim of Lua Poholo, a deep secondary crater. There is no warning of Lua Poholo's fragile edge — a hazard during poor visibility. After climbing the east side of the caldera rim, follow the trail to reach Mauna Loa Cabin in about 1.5 more miles.

HIKING AREA NO. 2
Saddle Road

The center of the Island of Hawaii is dominated by the great twin shield volcanoes, Mauna Loa, "long mountain," and Mauna Kea, "white mountain." The 6,600-foot-high saddle between them, with Mauna Loa to the south and Mauna Kea to the north, has been repeatedly covered and built up by massive lava flows running down the side of Mauna Loa. The Saddle Road, Highway 200, from Hilo follows up the course of the lava flow of 1855 and over the Saddle to reach the leeward side of the island.

With eternal optimism, ferns, shrubs, and trees spread over the barren new lava, more slowly in higher, drier, and cooler areas and more quickly in wetter and warmer areas. Inevitably new flows flood down, burn all before them, and the process starts once more. The flank of Mauna Kea and cinder cones, such as Puu Huluhulu, stand green and untouched while the tides of lava rise at their feet.

At the 5,000-6,000-foot level on the Saddle, the wet, cool areas of native Hawaiian forest are traversed by the Kaumana and Puu Oo Trails. These trails lead across a sea of lava with occasional kipukas, which are islands of vegetation missed by surrounding lava flows. The depredations of livestock seem to be less complete in these regions and these kipukas, for now, are above the range of mosquitoes in Hawaii.

At lower elevations the native Hawaiian birds have already been mostly destroyed by avian malaria and pox spread by mosquitoes. However, within these charmed circles one may still observe much of the original flora and fauna, including rare native Hawaiian birds.

Puu Huluhulu Cinder Cone at 6,758 feet on the crest of the Saddle rises above the surrounding sea of barren lava like an island fortress, preserving its small forest. It is a short, easy hike; the better for the fact that it is little used.

There are no campgrounds in the Saddle area. However, cabins at the Mauna Kea State Recreation Area (Pohakuloa) high on the cool crest of the Saddle may be rented from the Division of State Parks, P.O. Box 936, Hilo, HI 96720-0849, telephone (808) 933-4221. This is a good base for exploring the area and is a source of water. The weather, though cool, is drier than Hilo, the stars are clear at night, and there are no mosquitoes. The mornings are usually clear but as the day progresses clouds tend to climb up from Hilo.

The trails are short enough for day hikes to be combined with tours across the island. However, it should be noted that some rental car companies make the Saddle Road off limits for their cars, even though it is paved.

Cabin at Mauna Kea State Recreation Area

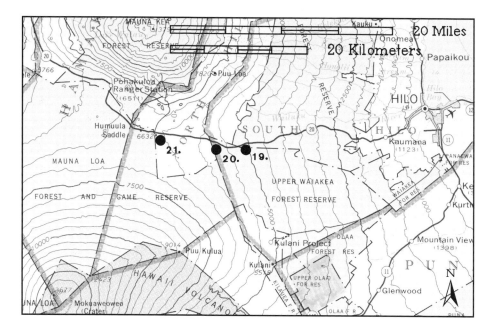

19. Kaumana Trail

Saddle Road
2 hours, round trip
500 calories; easier
3.2 miles, round trip
Highest point: 5243 feet
Lowest point: 4880 feet
Map: Upper Piihonua 1:24,000
Division of Forestry and Wildlife

Massive lava flows have repeatedly flooded down from Mauna Loa's northeast rift zone toward the high saddle between Mauna Kea and Mauna Loa, even in recent history. The topography causes flows to turn eastward toward Hilo after they reach the saddle. They spread over the land until the vents high on Mauna Loa stop supplying lava. The flows have so far stopped short of Hilo itself, but only in the narrow scope of human history.

A footnote to such great events is the Kaumana Trail, which follows the course of the 1855 lava flow. This pahoehoe flow has a smooth surface and a gentle, even slope, providing a natural route for a foot trail. Returning native vegetation, still not so thick as to greatly impede travel, has created scenes along the trail reminiscent of some well-tended garden of rocks, ferns, and mosses. One almost expects to round a corner and find the gardener at his work, to be greeted with ready praise.

Along the trail are kipukas (areas surrounded by lava flows) with ferns and older ohia trees, like islands in a river. They are the homes of native and exotic birds such as apapane, iiwi, housefinch, white eye, and leiothrix. The cause of the luxuriant foliage along the route is the heavy mist and rain that usually blankets the area, increasing as the day progresses.

Route: Both ends of the trail join the Saddle Road. It is best taken by starting at the upper end. The trailhead is on the

Nature's Garden

south side of the highway and is not well marked. However, as measured by the mileage signs along the side of the Saddle Road (Highway 200), it is 19.7 miles east of Hilo. The trail is marked by ahu (stone cairns), and there are old improvements on the trail, such as, small handmade causeways.

At first, the trail goes southerly on the level for 200 yards. The trail then climbs a minor rise near small kipukas. Upon reaching the top it turns gently downhill,

Amaumau Fern

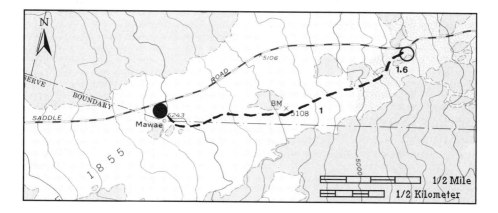

easterly, towards Hilo, and parallels the highway. This is the best portion of the trail for photography. At lower elevations it becomes wetter and more densely covered by vegetation.

The trail gently descends along the lava flow until at about 1.4 miles it passes between two kipukas as it turns north toward the highway. Soon the trail comes close to the highway at a point 18.4 west from Hilo. A somewhat overgrown extension of the trail continues down the lava flow beyond here. Return as you came, or to shorten the hike, arrange for a pick up from here.

20. Puu Oo Trail

Saddle Road

4 hours, round trip
1100 calories; harder
7.4 miles, round trip
Highest point: 5800 feet
Lowest point: 5750 feet
Maps: Kulani, Puu Oo, Upper Piihonua 1:24,000
Division of Forestry and Wildlife

A lovely belt of wet, native ohia forest, largely intact, grows at about the 2,000-6,000-foot level on windward Mauna Loa. The region with its thin soils could not be farmed and the grazing was poor. Thus, the forest has survived. Flows of smooth pahoehoe lava in some parts of this forest have covered large areas, creating easy natural walkways. The Puu Oo Trail traverses one such area in the forest reserves along the Saddle Road.

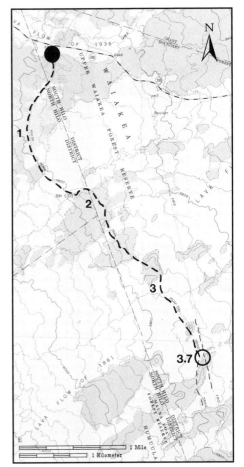

Early cattle ranchers in the saddle lands between Mauna Kea and Mauna Loa established the Puu Oo Trail to drive their herds around the beds of rough aa lava that blocked direct access to the seaport of Hilo. The trail led to the town of Volcano near Hawaii Volcanoes National Park. From there the cattle could be driven down the road to Hilo or, in still earlier times, to Keauhou Landing to the south. The trail has not been used for this purpose for many years. Yet, it may still be followed by looking closely for ahu (stone cairns) and other trail markers.

Since the trail is at nearly 6,000 feet, it can be cool and wet. The afternoon often brings sudden fog, rain, and cool temperatures. Rainfall in the area is up to 80 inches a year, but the land appears quite dry because of the good drainage of the underlying lava. There is no drinking water on the trail.

Route: Take the Saddle Road (Highway 200) west from Hilo until about 0.4 miles after the 22-mile marker, near the boundary of the Ainahou and the Upper Waiakea Forest Reserves. The trail begins on the left, south, side of the highway. A wooden sign may mark the trailhead.

Kipuka Forest

Follow the trail from the parking area south along a course roughly parallel to and west of a service road and a power-line, which are visible in the distance. The trail is difficult to follow at points. Look for ahu and be quick to retrace your steps if lost. The trail crosses the lava flows of 1855, 1881, and 1935, among others, which provide good examples of both rough aa and smooth pahoehoe lava. Thickness and type of vegetation varies on these well-drained flows depending on the age of the flow and the type of lava.

The trail also crosses large kipukas, where lava flows have by-passed older growth of ohia, pukiawe, ohelo, and majestic koa trees. These are populated with endemic and introduced species of birds. Native ferns, lichens, and mosses are found all along the way.

At about 3.7 miles the trail joins the powerline road, a good turnaround point. From here it is possible to return to the trailhead via the powerline road and the Saddle Road instead of retracing the trail. After reaching the highway, the trailhead is to the left.

21. Puu Huluhulu Trail
Saddle Road
1 hour, round trip
100 calories; easier
0.6 miles, round trip
Highest point: 6758 feet
Lowest point: 6560 feet
Map: Puu Oo 1:24,000
Division of Forestry and Wildlife

Puu Huluhulu is a cinder cone near the crest of the high saddle between Mauna Kea and Mauna Loa. It stands like a fortress island in a sea of pahoehoe lava and was, at one time, considered as the center point for a wall to divert flows of lava which periodically pour down from Mauna Loa's Northeast Rift Zone and threaten Hilo.

Puu Huluhulu is topped by native vegetation of species originally widespread at 6,000-7,000 feet on Mauna Kea. Its height saved its vegetation from the hot lava and, thus, it has become an island of relative preservation. Native birds, above the range of mosquitoes, still make the area their home, as also do birds of introduced species. Birds such as apapane, iiwi, house finch, leiothrix, wild turkey, and white eye flit among the trees, especially in the cooler parts of the day, when birds are more active.

A nature trail, constructed by the Youth Conservation Corps, leads through a remnant of the native forest, which includes specimens of sandalwood, koa, naio, mamani, and aalii. The trail to the top of the cinder cone, though overgrown and hard to find in places, is not difficult. The top of Puu Huluhulu can be a pleasant place for a picnic, especially in the spring when the plants are at their best. It is a fine perch to watch the afternoon clouds creeping up like a rising sea from the direction of Hilo. The crumbly top of the cinder

Atop Puu Huluhulu

quarry on the northwest side should be avoided.

Route: Take the Saddle Road (Highway 200) from Hilo for about 27 miles. The turnoff to the trailhead is on the left, south, side of the road. The trailhead is 0.1 miles from the turnoff, on the right hand side.

The trail starts at two points up a small side cone lying on the east side of the main cone. The side cone has good examples of plants which grow on well-drained lava with little soil development. The two branches soon come together to form one trail. This trail descends slightly, passing through thick koa forest growing in deeper soil.

The trail climbs to the north side of the main cone and leads around it to the northwest side of the cone. There is a heavy growth of false staghorn fern (uluhe). Eventually the trail reaches a bare area

Puu Huluhulu

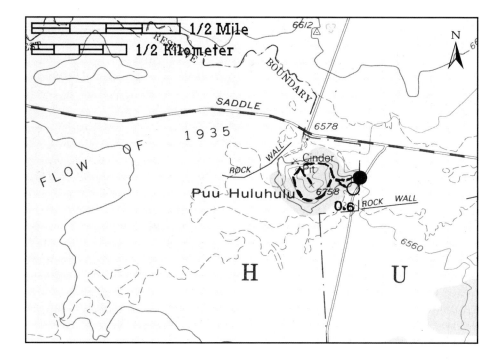

where earth moving equipment used in connection with the cinder pit operation on the northwest side of the cone has removed vegetation. The trail then continues circling the cone to its south side. Side trails lead to the top of the cone.

After completely circling the cone and going, in part, through thick false staghorn fern, the trail rejoins the route that led around the north side. Descend to return to the trailhead.

HIKING AREA NO. 3
Hilo Area and Hamakua Coast

Water and the passage of much time since the last volcanic activity have made the windward sides of Mauna Kea and Kohala differ greatly from the rest of the Big Island. The flows of lava, older here than elsewhere on the island and exposed to more water, have had a chance to decompose into soil. The rich soil holds water and allows the growth of the luxuriant vegetation through which the trails in this area pass. Streams cutting through lava beds of varying strengths give rise to spectacular waterfalls and deep valleys. Great sea cliffs have been formed because the surf has had time to cut into the flank of the dying volcanoes, uninterrupted by new flows of lava.

Hawaii Tropical Botanical Garden, in a lovely setting among the sea cliffs, has a large collection of plants from all over the tropical world. Gentle trails wind through the garden past the flowers and streams.

The easy Akaka Falls Trail in Akaka Falls State Park shows classic Hawaiian waterfalls and the richness of the plant life the region can support. Though the scenery is what most people think of as Hawaiian, the magnificent plant life consists almost entirely of species new to the Hawaiian Islands.

The Kalopa Native Forest Nature Trail in Kalopa State Park loops through a remnant of the magnificent native forest which once covered the region. The slash and burn agriculture of the ancient

Plantation Eucalyptus

Hawaiians, livestock brought by Europeans, and land clearing for sugar production destroyed almost all of the native forest. Near the park are vigorous groves of introduced eucalyptus, paperbark, silk oak, and ironwood planted in an early conservation effort. These are crisscrossed by several trails, with a route joining them, described here as the Kalopa Gulch Loop.

The trail from Waipio to Waimanu Valley goes along the base of the Kohala

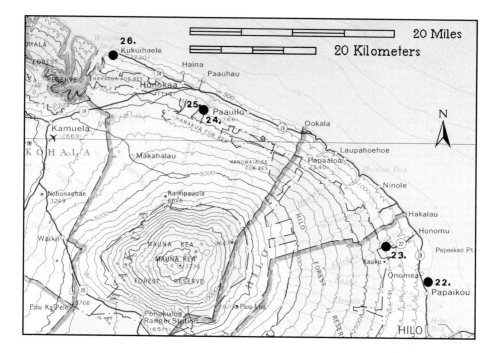

Mountains, the oldest on Hawaii. The valleys were once densely populated but are now quite remote. The flat alluvial floors of the Waipio and Waimanu Valleys were formed when this part of the island sank and slowing mountain streams dropped their loads of sediment. The trail passes through forest and across many small streams. Near the end, it drops down into Waimanu Valley, which has been made into a National Estuarine Research Reserve administered by the Division of Forestry and Wildlife.

The campground and rental cabins at Kalopa State Park make a good base for exploring the area. The Hamakua Coast is somewhat wet, but is green and pleasant. The Division of Forestry and Wildlife provides the permits for the wilderness camping at a shelter part way along the trail and at long and beautiful, black-sand Waimanu Beach.

Waimanu Beach

22. Hawaii Tropical Botanical Garden
Hilo Area
1-3 hours, round trip
100 calories; easiest
0.7 miles, round trip
Highest point: 40 feet
Lowest point: sea level
Map: Papaikou 1:24,000
Hawaii Tropical Botanical Garden; admission charge

There are many places of interest and beauty in Hawaii, but rarely are they what visitors imagine a proper tropical paradise should be. Hawaii Tropical Botanical Garden, a little north of Hilo, is one of the few places that comes close to the image of the lost Eden of brilliant flowers, waterfalls, pounding white surf, and general luxuriance which many visitors expect to find. The garden is bounded by green, forested hills and the black rocks and brilliant white breakers of Onomea Bay. From 1820 to 1870 the bay was used as a landing for sailing ships bringing cargo to and from the Onomea Sugar Mill.

The garden includes over 2,000 species of palms, bromeliads, gingers, and other plants, some quite rare. Streams with spilling waterfalls cross it and gentle paths wind through the garden among the collections of plants gathered from all over the tropical world. Many are of extraordinary beauty. Plants have been labelled to show the family, genus, species, and country of origin. Photography in Hawaii is usually best in early morning or late in the afternoon, but in the garden it is best toward mid-day when the sun has attained its greatest height. Then the glossy foliage appears with brilliant greens above and darkest shade below, with a profusion of new and brightly colored blossoms. Flashes and high speed film are useful.

Route: From Hilo, take Highway 19 north along the coast. Just past the seven-

Onomea Falls

mile mark the highway reaches a school on the left and passes beneath a pedestrian overpass. Just beyond these, a sign on the right marks the beginning of a four-mile scenic route seaward of the main highway. Follow the scenic route about 1 mile to the offices of Hawaii Tropical Botanical Garden, where you need to park. From Kona, drive through Waimea, then follow Highway 19 south toward Hilo. About five miles after passing the towns of Hakalau and Honomu a blue sign on the

Garden Path

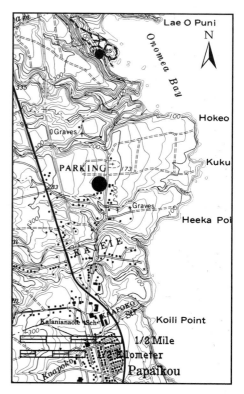

right will say "Scenic Route 4 Miles Long." Turn left near the sign and continue on the scenic route about three miles to the office and bookstore of Hawaii Tropical Botanical Garden. Park nearby. Transportation from hotels in Hilo may be arranged through the garden, telephone (808) 964-5233, P.O. Box 1415, Hilo, HI 96721.

An admission fee, paid at the office and bookstore, is charged for the support of the non-profit, 501(c)(3), garden foundation. The garden is open daily from about 9:00 a.m. to 4:30 p.m. A mini-bus shuttles visitors from the bookstore down the narrow cliff road to Onomea Bay and the garden. Trail guide pamphlets at the garden describe the little winding paths and labeled plantings in detail. The area can be showery and has the usual allotment of lowland mosquitoes, which seem to be readily discouraged by repellant. Allow plenty of time for taking the garden paths since there is much to see.

23. Akaka Falls Trail
Hilo Area
1/2 hour, loop trip
75 calories; easiest
0.5 miles, loop trip
Highest point: 1200 feet
Lowest Point: 1100 feet
Map: Akaka Falls 1:24,000
Division of State Parks

Views of Akaka and Kahuna Falls and a walk through the dense, wet forest of the type found at low elevations on the windward side of Hawaii make this leisurely half-hour hike a favorite. The easy, well-maintained trail, with steps in the steeper portions, winds gently down to skirt the edge of the deep canyon into which Akaka and Kahuna Falls spill.

Both Kahuna and Akaka Falls were formed because of the variations in strength of the layers of rock underlying them. Lava flows are typically more solid toward the center and often have soft layers of weathered rock or dirt between flows. The softer layers of rock decompose and erode more rapidly than the hard layers. Hard upper layers are undercut when the soft layers below them are eroded by streams. The unsupported solid layers fall off in large chunks into pools below, are broken up, and are then carried away by the plunging waters. In this way, Akaka Falls and others like it have moved upstream over the years, building deep canyons.

The dense and varying vegetation along the trail is in itself a sufficient reason for a visit. Even in wet weather this trail is worth taking since the occasional breaks in the mist around the falls only add to the air of beauty and mystery of the location. In addition the fragrant scents of the rain forest and flowers growing along the trail are much stronger on rainy days.

Akaka Falls

Route: Drive about eleven miles north from Hilo on Highway 19 to Highway 220, which ends in 3.7 miles at Akaka Falls State Park. Overnight camping is not allowed. The loop trail begins at the state park parking lot. It may be followed either clockwise or counterclockwise.

The counterclockwise route leads first to Kahuna Falls (a kahuna is a priest of the ancient Hawaiian religion). It cascades from a side canyon opposite into the main canyon below, making several drops into

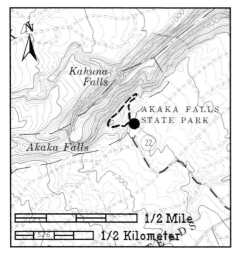

Forest Stream

plunge pools. After the view overlooking Kahuna Falls and a short climb, the trail comes to the superb vista overlooking Akaka Falls (akaka means clear or luminous). At scenic points the Division of State Parks has built benches as resting places.

The trail weaves through rainy forest made up almost entirely of plants brought by man to Hawaii. Epiphytes (non-parasitic plants growing on other plants) hang from the forest canopy. Brilliant red ginger, fragrant plumeria, banana plants, ti plants, bamboo, and the colorful flowers of the bird of paradise delight the senses. The muffled sound of falling water and the soft smells of plants blend into the mists. White vapour, cool to the touch, curls up from the canyons. Birds call, unseen in the forest.

The trail returns to the parking area through huge philodendrons which stand guard with their 2-foot leaves, making the hiker feel like an insect in the greenery. At the top of the trail are well-maintained restrooms, a drinking fountain, and picnic tables with orchids hanging overhead.

24. Kalopa Gulch Loop

Hamakua Coast

2 hours, loop trip
500 calories; easier
2.7 miles, loop trip
Highest point: 2530 feet
Lowest point: 2080 feet
Map: Honokaa 1:24,000
Division of Forestry and Wildlife
    and Division of State Parks

The dreams of men live on, now visible, in Kalopa's planted groves. The Kalopa section of the Hamakua Forest Reserve, laid bare by overgrazing, was reforested in the 1930's. The goals of reforestation at this time were to retard soil erosion and protect watersheds. Native plant species were not used since they were considered expensive, slow growing, and unlikely to survive. In Kalopa, fast-growing intro-duced species, such as, blue gum, paper bark, silk oak, and ironwood were select-ed because they would have no commer-cial stumpage value to tempt future gener-ations. The one exception was swamp mahogany, which was thought to have value for timber. Years later, according to plan, the alien forest, except for the swamp mahogany, has been left untouched and the soil has been saved. Unplanned, a native understory is re-establishing itself.

Next to this planted forest, Kalopa State Park and Recreation Area has cabins, water, cooking facilities, campsites, picnic spots, the beginnings of an arboretum of Hawaii's native plants, and an excellent nature trail through native forest. Groups can be accommodated. Write to the Division of State Parks for cabin use and camping permits: 75 Aupuni St., Hilo, HI 96720, telephone (808) 933-4200. The area tends to be rainy.

Route: Drive about 40 miles up the Mamalahoa Highway (Highway 19) northwest from Hilo or about three miles southeast of Honokaa. There is a signed turnoff leading inland to Kalopa. Take and follow the signs 3-4 miles uphill to the recreation area.

The Kalopa Gulch Loop links parts of several trails traversing the planted forest. The trailhead is on the left (east) side about 200 yards up the road from the entrance to the recreation area and about the same distance down the road from the guest cabin area. The first leg of the loop is called Robusta Lane. It leads on a level course east, toward the steep edge of Kalopa Gulch 0.3 miles away.

When the loop trail reaches the edge of Kalopa Gulch it turns right to follow it uphill, passing turnoffs onto Blue Gum and Silk Oak Lanes along the way. The trail passes large and thriving eucalyptus, with their squeaking branches, rustling leaves, and medicinal odor, which is offensive to mosquitoes. After 1.3 miles from its start the loop trail passes by rustling paper bark trees and tree ferns, and then swings right, west, onto Ironwood Lane.

After going on the level through 0.2 miles of sighing ironwoods the trail reach-es an abandoned and overgrown jeep road. The usual course of the loop is to descend on this road for 1.2 miles to the trailhead.

Start of the Loop

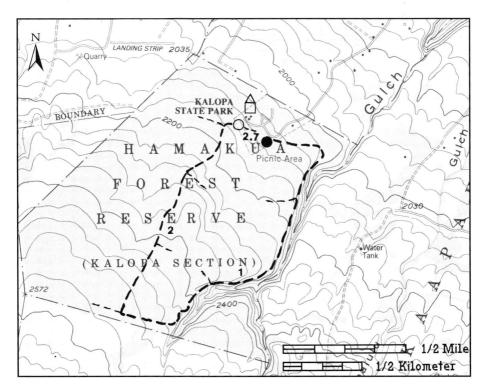

25. Kalopa Native Forest Nature Trail
Hamakua Coast
1 hour, loop trip
100 calories; easiest
0.7 miles, loop trip
Highest point: 2190 feet
Lowest point: 2090 feet
Map: Honokaa 1:24,000
Division of State Parks

The native Hawaiian forest which once mantled the wet Hamakua District is almost gone. At Kalopa State Park is a 100 acre remnant, saved from conversion to cane fields in the 1960's by the efforts of Dr. P. Quentin Tomich and other far-sighted individuals.

An exceptionally well-written and insightful pamphlet describing the plants and animals along the trail and the biology of the forest may be available at the trailhead. It tells the remarkable story of the native forest, a story still unfolding.

The forest here is a borderland of native and alien plants and animals. The succession of species is a slow process. Often in Hawaii the alien species win out, especially, if aided by man. But this forest demonstrates that the native Hawaiian forest can come back, if spared man-caused disturbances. It is an important lesson to ponder.

As the sugar industry becomes unprofitable in Hawaii, consideration may be given to converting fields back to forest. The success of the native forest in Kalopa gives evidence that, if protected from alien influences such as pigs, cattle and fire, the native species may be suitable for replanting.

The Kalopa State Park and Recreation area has cabins, water, cooking facilities, campsites, picnic spots, and the beginnings of an arboretum of Hawaii's native plants. Write to the Division of State Parks for cabin use and camping permits at 75

Native Forest

Aupuni St., Hilo, HI 96720, telephone (808) 933-4200. The area tends to be rainy.

Route: Drive about 40 miles up the Mamalahoa Highway (Highway 19) northwest from Hilo or about 3 miles southeast of Honokaa. There is a signed turnoff leading inland to the park. Take it and follow the signs 3-4 miles uphill to the park and the cabins at the end of the road.

The trailhead for the nature trail is about 100 yards, from the park cabins, nearly on

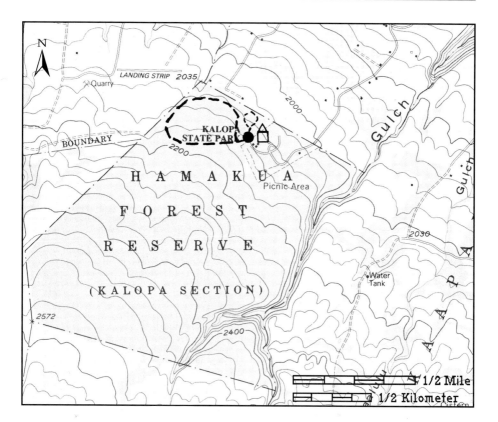

the level across the lawn. The route to the trailhead passes by an access trail leading down into the arboretum for an interesting side trip.

The nature trail soon passes into deep, dark forest. The upper canopy is mostly ancient ohia trees, some exceptionally large. Beneath them is an understory of tree ferns, hame, kolea, kopiko, olomea, pilo, ground ferns, and other native plants. The short-lived, alien guava, with their smooth skins, are in the process of dying out, since the forest is too dark for their seedlings. The deepening shade from the native species puts the weedy guava at a disadvantage. Here and there other exotics, such as strangler fig, still seem to hold on. The forest floor is little disturbed by the occasional incursions of pigs which root up the soil in their search for worms and roots. Under this regime of minor distur-

bance to the soil, the native plants can gradually increase, the weedy aliens such as thimbleberry do not gain new footholds, and the tide of extinction is held back.

Wandering through the ancient and the planted forests of Kalopa one may observe and compare them with each other and the surrounding lands, consider the past, and imagine the future.

26. Waipio and Waimanu Valleys (Muliwai Trail)

Hamakua Coast
2-3 days, round trip
7 hours in; 8 hours out
5800 calories; hardest
18 miles, round trip
Highest point: 1350 feet
Lowest point: sea level
Maps: Honokane, Kukuihaele 1:24,000
Division of Forestry and Wildlife

Waipio and Waimanu Valleys on the Hamakua Coast, rich in taro, were once centers of Hawaiian population. Imagination conjures up sights of feather-robed chieftains, confident in their authority, the armies of Kamehameha the Great, and the naval battle between the forces of Hawaii and Maui off Waimanu Valley. Today, few live in Waipio. Waimanu has become a National Estuarine Research Reserve to protect and study Hawaiian plants and animals.

The trail on the high plateau between Waipio and Waimanu crosses numerous streams then descends steeply into Waimanu Valley. In winter and during storms the streams run high and fords should not be attempted. Beware of surf, floods, pigs, pig hunters, and untreated water. Mosquitoes are plentiful and hungry. The trail can be steep, deeply eroded, rocky, muddy, and slippery. Good hiking boots with new threads are needed. Only experienced hikers should attempt it.

Camping is allowed at an uninviting open-sided shelter two-thirds of the way along the trail and in Waimanu, at several sites near the black sand beach, the area with fewest mosquitoes. Obtain camping permits from the Division of Forestry and Wildlife, 1643 Kilauea Ave., Hilo, HI 96720, telephone (808) 933-4221 or the Kamuela State Tree Nursery. The Waipio Treehouse, on the valley floor, offers comfortable lodging and a base for exploring the region, P.O. Box 5086, Honokaa, HI

Waiilikahi Falls

96727, telephone (808) 775-7160.

Route: From Hilo, take the Mamalahoa Highway (Highway 19) north for about 40 miles to Highway 240. Follow it through Honokaa 9.5 miles to its end at Waipio Valley Lookout. A paved 4-wheel-drive road, too steep for ordinary cars, descends the east slope of the valley. At 0.7 miles on the valley floor, take the first road on the right to the beach.

Follow the beach to ford Wailoa Stream, if safe. The best ford may be close to the ocean; however, its best spot may

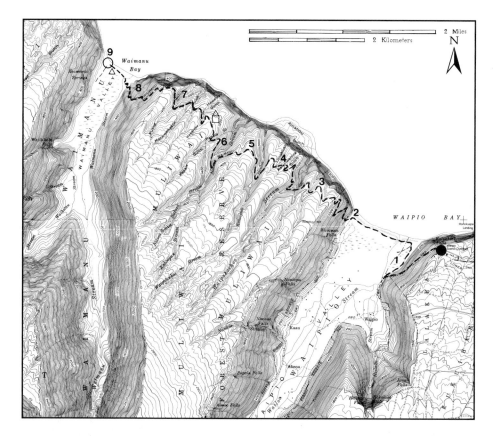

vary. After about half a mile along the beach and within 100 yards of the northwest wall of the valley, the trail leads up the valley floor past a swampy area into the forest below the wall. Soon the trail starts up a switchbacking ascent of the wall. Though rough and steep, the trail is well dug in and less difficult than it looks from the Waipio Valley Lookout. Here and elsewhere rain makes the footing slick and hazardous.

The trail attains the plateau on the northwest side of Waipio Valley and soon passes a small waterfall and pool. It contours along numerous small gulches and through native forest mixed with exotics such as ironwood and false kamani. It passes the camping shelter at 6.5 miles and reaches the steep and rugged descent to Waimanu Valley at about 8 miles.

Upon reaching the valley floor, work toward the beach through groves of hala trees. To reach the designated campsites in the ironwood along the beach, you must first ford Waimanu Stream, if safe, on the southeast end of the beach.

From the campsites a good side trip and the best source of water (treat it) is up the northwest side of the valley floor. The unmarked route passes through groves of mountain apple trees, often laden with tasty fruit, to Waiilikahi Falls, the first falls visible from the beach, and its deep, wide pool.

HIKING AREA NO.4
South Kona Coast

Kona, on the leeward, dry side of the island is well known for its fine hotels, golf courses, and sunshine. However, it has much rain on its slopes between 2,000 and 6,000 feet and trails lead to a variety of landscapes. The Big Island, unlike the others in the chain, makes some of its own weather. When the air on the leeward island is warmed by the sun during the day, it rises and pulls in wet sea air. This wet air is cooled as it rises, forming rain clouds in the afternoon. Thus, the fertile soils of the area support rich agriculture and, in pre-contact times, made the area home to a large population. Next to the sea the weather remains dry and balmy. The ancient Hawaiians could gather food from the mountainside and the sea, happily pursuing the arts of war and peace from their villages along the coast.

Puuhonua-o-Honaunau, with its great stone walls, and Kealakekua Bay, Cook's fateful anchorage, are in the heart of Kona. At Puuhonua-o-Honaunau are the overlapping trails of the pre-contact period and of the nineteenth century kingdom. The little-travelled trail to the Captain Cook Monument follows the nineteenth century kingdom road from near the town of Captain Cook to the clear waters of Kealakekua Bay. The soil-covered area to the south of the trail was a dryland agricultural complex supplying the chiefs at Kaawaloa and the priests at Napoopoo.

Manuka Natural Area Reserve near the

Captain Cook Monument

southeast rift zone of Mauna Loa, with its huge flows of lava and thin soils, was protected from man's influences because of its lack of economic value. It has now been set aside to preserve one of the best remnants of the mixed forest which once covered much larger areas of Hawaii. The reserve extends from wet ohia forests in its upper elevations through drier and drier forest and finally to barren coastal lava landscape.

The Manuka Nature Trail wanders

Coconut Palms — Puuhonua-o-Honaunau

through the rich native forest of the reserve, sublime in its silence. The Kaheawai Trail leads down toward the dry, barren, and starkly beautiful coast where the authority of man diminishes in the face of the works of nature.

Manuka Wayside along Highway 11 has an open shelter, which may be available for tent camping. There is no drinking water. Camping permits must be obtained from the Division of State Parks in Hilo.

In addition to the numerous resort accomodations of Kailua-Kona, there are modestly priced hotels in this hiking area, which make good bases for hiking. The Manago Hotel, with the flavor of an earlier Hawaii and an exceptionally good, moderately priced restaurant, remains the author's favorite.

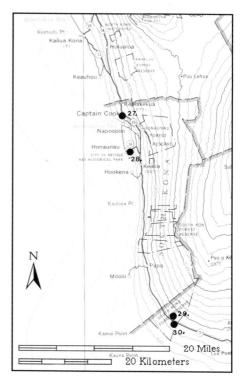

27. Captain Cook Monument via Kaawaloa Road

South Kona Coast

4 hours, round trip
1100 calories; harder
4.0 miles, round trip
Highest point: 1280 feet
Lowest point: sea level
Map: Honaunau 1:24,000
Division of State Parks

Captain Cook, the Great Navigator, was a decent man, much interested in the advancement of science and medicine, but his tall sailing ships and those that followed were veritable Pandora's boxes, carrying the agents of change and death. The goats, sheep, horses, cattle, large pigs and new plants which European ships brought made short work of much of the landscape. Diseases new to the islands decimated the Hawaiians.

The Captain Cook Monument stands next to the clear waters of Kealakekua Bay, the scene of his death in 1779. The trail to it follows the course of a road built about 1840 during the years of the Hawaiian Kingdom. The road was once important to the district as the only wagon access to Kaawaloa settlement and the key freighter landing by it, where his monument now stands.

Route: Take Highway 11 from Kailua-Kona south to Highway 160 near mile marker 11, just north of the town of Captain Cook. Turn right, downhill, at the turnoff. At 0.1 miles a dirt road goes down toward the ocean and the north side of Kealakekua Bay. Park at the turnoff. Hike a hundred yards down the dirt road and continue on the trail which is also a 4-wheel-drive road. It starts just after a private dirt road leads right. The grass on the trail may be heavy, but rock walls and brush on both sides define the route.

In a mile the trail reaches dry, open

A Cook Descendant in a Pensive Moment

flows of aa lava, nears the pali, and becomes more obviously a road. It passes south of Cook's Heiau (Puhina o Lono Heiau, lit. burning of Lono Heiau). It stands 50 yards above the trail. It was here that Cook was prepared for burial.

Cook had tried to hold a chief in Kaawaloa ransom for the return of a boat. The Hawaiians, not being the most passive of peoples, resisted this attempt. In the scuffle, Cook and four of his landing party were slain. The rest reached the

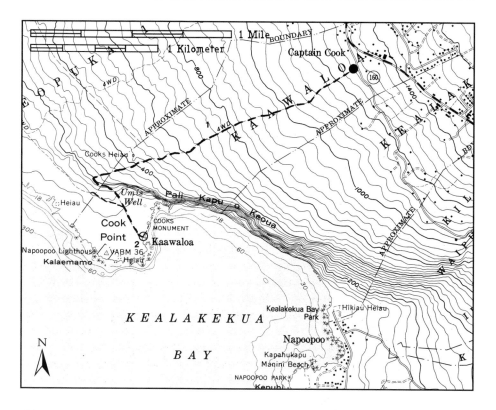

ships with luck and difficulty. Upset by this treatment, Cook's crew later fired on the settlement, convincing the Hawaiians to return portions of his remains.

Before Cook's death and against his wishes, a crueler punishment of the Hawaiians had begun when his sailors brought syphillis and other diseases ashore on Niihau. In later years missionaries were mindful of the spread of such illnesses. Perhaps discerning a useful connection between economic progress and the wages of sin, they encouraged passage of laws by which adulterers were sentenced to work on road gangs. These unfortunates, along with other law breakers and those too poor to pay their taxes in cash, built the Kingdom's roads.

The lonely road swings left toward the bay and then goes down the pali on a stone ramp. The ramp shows the superb dry masonry of the old Hawaiians, its

stones enduring monuments to master masons and dangerous liaisons, all long forgotten.

At the bottom of the pali the road splits. The branch to the monument leads straight toward the bay with its crystal waters and boat-loads of frolicking tourists. The spot where Cook was killed is marked by a small plaque to the left of the road's end, a few yards offshore. The large cement obelisk honoring Cook is 200 yards toward the cliffs, along the shore. It is framed by kiawe trees, said to be descendants of a single seed planted on Oahu in 1828, and surrounded landward by the silent stone walls of deserted habitations.

28. Puuhonua-o-Honaunau
South Kona Coast
1 hour, loop trip
150 calories; easiest
1.6 miles, loop trip
Highest point: 40 feet
Lowest point: sea level
Map: Honaunau 1:24,000
Puuhonua-o-Honaunau National Historical Park

Puuhonua-o-Honaunau National Park preserves the ancient ruins of heiau, fish ponds, house foundations, sled ramps, trails from different periods of Hawaiian history, and a great stone wall within whose boundaries kapu breakers and the vanquished could find refuge. From the visitor center a short, modern interpretive trail meanders by the impressive stone ruins, replicas of ancient buildings, and fearsome wooden carvings.

Beyond the interpretive area, lie the routes of an early foot path and a well-preserved 1871 horse trail leading south to a stone ramp over Keanaee Cliff. The cliff was on the route mentioned in Mark Twain's letters about the area. In the early days Keanaee Cliff, with its "frozen waterfall" of lava, was an obstacle to travelers along this coast, passable only at a low point where the cliff meets Alahaka Bay. The prehistoric foot trail, marked by a single row of smooth stones, reached the cliff at this low point after hugging the coast to avoid dreaded kapu areas inland.

With the introduction of horses and the end of the kapu system, the new, direct, inland horse trail was built, marked by "kerbstones" on either side and covered in parts with coral gravel. The substantial ramp now climbing the cliff was built around 1868 (See, *Trails* by Russell A. Apple, Bishop Museum Press).

Route: Take Highway 11 from Kailua-Kona south about 10 miles to Highway 160.

Go down Highway 160 steeply about four miles to the shore and the park visitor center.

To reach the courses of the ancient footpath and the 19th century kerbstone horse trail further south, walk along the road from the visitor center parking area toward the seaside picnic area. The modern road crosses the 19th century kerbstone road before reaching the picnic area. Note this for your return.

From the picnic area, walk south and along the shore for about a third of a mile. This follows the approximate course of the ancient foot trail, though little evidence of it is visible. Where the shoreline is indented by little Alahaka Bay, walk inland 100 paces to join the level 1871 horse trail, apparent from its white coral surfacing and kerbstones. Proceed south to climb the ramp. Beyond the ramp, the trail eventually passes out of the park area.

Return via the 1871 trail. It leads straight north from the ramp providing a good return route, passing by prospering introduced dryland plants which, being unpalatable, thorny, or poisonous, have defied the appetites of goats and cattle. The trail soon crosses the course of a rock sled ramp seen lying uphill on the right. When covered with pili grass and dirt in ancient times the ramp must have been the scene of many a merry slide. In an act eloquently bespeaking the new age, the royal sled ramp was torn apart to provide fill rock for the horse trail.

Kapu

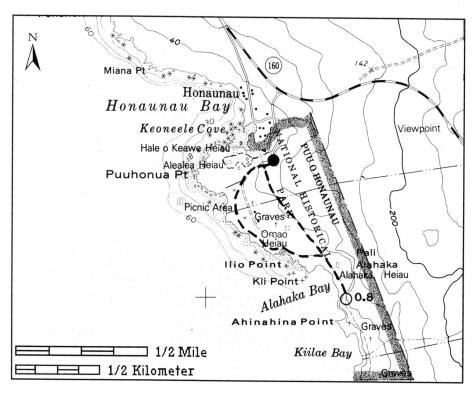

29. Manuka Nature Trail

South Kona Coast
2-3 hours, loop trip
300 calories; easier
2.1 miles, loop trip
Highest point: 2280 feet
Lowest point: 1790 feet
Map: Pohue Bay 1:24,000
Division of Forestry and Wildlife
  and Division of State Parks

The 25,000 acre Manuka Natural Area Reserve in South Kona has been set aside to preserve a broad range of ecosystems. The reserve extends from wet ohia forest in its upper elevations down to drier and drier forest and finally to the barren coastal lava plain. It has the best remnant of the mixed forest which once ranged into the wet uplands and the dry lowlands over larger areas of the island. A wide variety of native trees are found in the area, including aulu, kolea, kopiko, mamaki, ohia, olomea, olopua, and papala. Mixed in are later arrivals such as avocado, coffee, kukui, guava, and ti plants.

The Manuka Nature Trail leads from Manuka State Wayside on the north side of Highway 11 into the wet forest. Adjacent to Manuka Wayside is an arboretum containing many species of native trees. Manuka Wayside has no drinking water, but does have an open shelter available for tent camping on cement slabs. Camping permits must be obtained from the Division of State Parks, which also has an excellent brochure on the Manuka Natural Area Reserve.

Route: Take Highway 11 (Mamalahoa Highway) about 40 miles south from Kailua-Kona or 81.3 miles from Hilo to Manuka State Wayside. From the parking lot, the trail starts into the forest, across the park's lawn, directly toward the center of the island. The trail travels generally northeast for about a mile.

On its pleasant, fairly level course through the usually damp mixed forest, the Manuka Nature Trail passes over flows of rough aa lava from 2,000 to 4,000 years old, covered with fern, moss, and lichen. When the rain patters on the leaves it makes a sound like rushing water.

As the trail turns left, it reaches the edge of a large crater in the recesses of the forest. The crater floor is inaccessible to pigs. Because of this the native plants there are unusually abundant. Much of the destruction of Hawaii's native plants and birds is caused by pigs, tearing up the ground seeking worms and roots. Fast-growing, weedy, introduced plants are able to take root in the disturbed areas and crowd out the natives. Small pools of water form in places that have been rooted up, creating breeding pools for mosquitoes. Mosquitoes spread avian malaria and avian pox which cause the native birds to die painfully and drive whole species toward extinction.

After the trail passes the crater it loops to descend to the northwestern corner of the grass-covered area of the arboretum and the state wayside. Though the area is not cold, expect rain along the trail, especially later in the day as the air warmed by the sun on the Kona Coast rises up the mountain and begins to condense.

Tree Fern

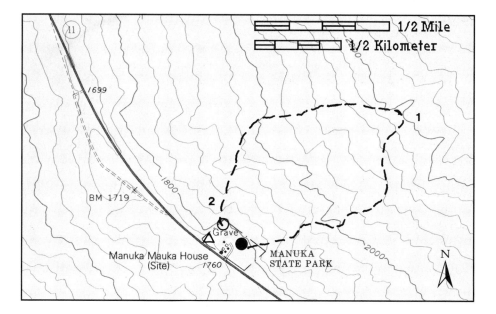

30. Kaheawai Trail
South Kona Coast
5 hours, round trip
1000 calories; harder
6.4 miles, round trip
Highest point: 1930 feet
Lowest point: 660 feet
Map: Pohue Bay 1:24,000
Division of Forestry and Wildlife

The Manuka Natural Area Reserve extends from a wet ohia forest in its upper regions through a drier mixed forest down to barren coastal lava plain.

The Keawahai Trail begins on the south side of the reserve on Highway 11 and leads into increasing drier areas. It follows the edge of a large lava channel down toward the coast. The trail becomes too difficult to find at about 3.2 miles from the start, shortly after it crosses a natural arch over the lava channel. This description stops at that point, though one could chart out a rough, unmarked, waterless course to the coast. Ample water should be carried since there is none on the trail and the region can be hot.

Route: Take Highway 11 (Mamalahoa Highway) south about 40 miles from Kailua-Kona to 1.5 miles east of Manuka Wayside. This is 79.8 miles from Hilo. The trailhead is on the extreme east side of the Reserve, high on the embankment on the south side of Highway 11. Since the official trailhead is located awkwardly on the high south embankment, hikers have, instead, followed the course of a dirt road beginning about 150 yards east on Highway 11.

The dirt road reaches the Reserve and the route follows the gradually descending continuation of the dirt road, alongside the deep lava channel on the right. The road soon changes to a trail, perhaps marked by tapes.

Trailhead

The route may not be well-marked, but it follows along the smooth pahoehoe lava that has spilled over the side of the lava channel. If one drifts off the trail too far to the left, there is usually rough aa lava; too far to the right, the cliff along the edge of the lava channel prevents passage. The route is especially good for bird watching since the tops of the trees growing from the somewhat wetter floor of the lava channel are near eye level making the birds easily visible.

As one descends, the landscape becomes gradually drier. The trees become smaller and are further apart, however, larger in the lava channel. As the land becomes fairly barren the trail reaches the natural arch over the lava channel. There are good views here of the desolate coast fringed by rootless cones piled up by lava flows exploding in the sea. This is a good turnaround place since beyond the arch

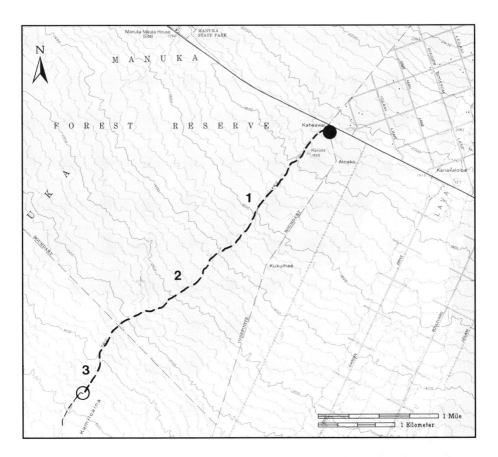

the trail is almost nonexistent and the land
is covered by rough aa lava.

The Arch

The lights begin to twinkle from
*   the rocks;*
The long day wanes; the slow
*   moon climbs; the deep*
Moans round with many voices.
*   Come, my friends.*
'T is not too late to seek a newer
*   world.*
Push off, and sitting well in order
*   smite*
The sounding furrows; for my
*   purpose holds*
To sail beyond the sunset, and
*   the baths*
Of all the western stars, until I die.

—Alfred, Lord Tennyson
Ulysses

The Last Hill — Kaaha Trail

Index

Order Form

The Fernglen Press

473 Sixth Street, Suite B
Lake Oswego, Oregon 97034, USA
Telephone (503) 635-4719
Fax (503) 635-5468

QUANTITY   AMOUNT

Please, send me the following books by Craig Chisholm:

_____ *Hawaiian Hiking Trails,*
             The Guide for All of the Islands, $15.95   _____

_____ *Kauai Hiking Trails,* $12.95   _____

_____ *Hawaii, the Big Island, Hiking Trails,* $12.95   _____

Also, use this form to order the companion travel guides:

_____ *Kauai, a Paradise Family Guide,* $12.95
             by Don and Bea Donohugh   _____

_____ *Hawaii the Big Island,*
             a Paradise Family Guide, $12.95
             by John Penisten   _____

_____ *Maui and Lanai, a Paradise Family Guide,* $12.95
             by Greg and Christie Stilson   _____

Total for books   _____

Shipping:

First book $2.00   _____

Each add'l book   .50   _____

Air Mail each book $4.00   _____

AMOUNT ENCLOSED (U.S. funds)   _____

I understand that I may return any books for a full refund if not satisfied.

Name: _____

Address: _____

City: _____ State:_____ Zip: _____